Roaring Dorset!
Encounters with Big Cats

Roaring Dorset!
Encounters with Big Cats

Merrily Harpur

Roving
Press

Published by Roving Press Ltd
4 Southover Cottages, Frampton, Dorset, DT2 9NQ, UK
Tel: +44 (0)1300 321531
www.rovingpress.co.uk

First Published 2008 by Roving Press Ltd

ISBN: 978-1-906651-01-5

A catalogue record for this book is available from the British Library

Photographs by Merrily Harpur unless stated otherwise
Cover design by Tim Musk
Front cover picture © iStockphoto.com/Oliver Malms, VFKA
Back cover picture © iStockphoto.com/John Pitcher

Set in Minion 10.5/12.6 pt by Beamreach Printing (www.beamreachuk.co.uk)
Printed and bound in England by Beamreach Printing (www.beamreachuk.co.uk)

Contents

Preface

Dorset is the county in which you are, arguably, most likely to encounter an anomalous big cat – ABC for short. It is third in the county league table of sightings, just behind the bigger and more populous counties of Yorkshire and Lincolnshire – which means there are more sightings per head in the county than anywhere else in Britain.

The sightings described in this book give an idea of the huge range of ordinary country people who have come into contact with ABCs – from farmers, gamekeepers and deer stalkers to police officers, commuters, teachers, taxi drivers and ramblers; in fact anyone strolling around the countryside might intriguingly glimpse one.

This is not as alarming as it sounds, for British ABCs are very unlike the leopards, pumas and lynxes they are commonly assumed to be. They have differently coloured coats, are different shapes and sizes – and have very different manners and habits. Moreover, unlike big cats in their native countries it seems ours cannot be caught, or even photographed clearly; and although some have been implicated in livestock or deer kills, none has ever been known to attack human beings. In fact it is a truism among ABC researchers that if you want to be sure never to meet a British big cat, carry a camera.

What are they then? That is a mystery that four decades of research has been unable to solve. As the magazine *Fortean Times* put it: 'The glimpse of an ABC is now Britain's commonest brush with the unknown'. I hope this book will provoke some speculation of your own, or at the very least change your view of a landscape that can produce such beautiful and elusive creatures.

While *Roaring Dorset!* is the first serious and comprehensive book on the county's ABCs, it is primarily designed as an exciting read. I have kept the freshness and drama of the eyewitnesses' verbatim accounts, while the Introduction and Current Theories offer some new perspectives on what is often an amazing and always a strange experience – one that is, paradoxically, very common.

Merrily Harpur
July 2008

Acknowledgements

I am most grateful to the many eyewitnesses, named and unnamed, who took the time and trouble to contact me via my Dorset Big Cats Register website or emailed me. Their thoughtful and accurate reports have made this book possible, and are helping to draw up a national picture of the ABC phenomenon. Thanks also to Andy Elliott for help in drawing the map of sightings.

Big cats are no respecters of geographical demarcations, and I have included some sightings that occurred just outside the county boundary, but arbitrarily excluded others. Please contact me if you feel I have unfairly excluded yours! For reasons of space I have also had to leave out, this time around, many reports of suspicious animal kills, footprints, roars and growls, eyes shining at night and so forth. Again, if you feel I have been unfair please let me know and I will try to include more in later editions of the book. Finally I am very aware that despite my best efforts I will have missed out some reports completely, so if there are sightings or evidence of ABCs out there that I don't know of, please email me at research@dorsetbigcats.org – in complete confidence if necessary. To report sightings outside the county, please visit the *Big Cats in Britain* website, www.bigcatsinbritain.org.

Many thanks are also due to the Dorset Police, in particular PC John Snellin and our local PWLOs whose interest and helpfulness to both my research and the eyewitnesses is always exemplary.

I would like to thank the local press too, for their involvement in bringing many of the stories I quote to light – for instance the *Bournemouth Echo, Bridport and Lyme Regis News, Dorset Echo, Western Daily Press* and the *Western Gazette*. Their keen and interesting reportage has greatly contributed to the understanding of this mercurial subject and how it affects the lives of ordinary people.

Finally I would like to thank Mark Fraser, of *Big Cats in Britain*, for much inspiration, and whose generosity with his time and information seems to be limitless.

About the Author

Merrily Harpur is a freelance cartoonist, illustrator and writer and has contributed regular cartoons and feature articles to *The Guardian, The Financial Times, The Sunday Times, The Sunday Telegraph, Fortean Times, The Daily Mail, Private Eye, The Spectator, Country Living, The Field, Country Life* and other British and Irish national publications. Her work currently appears weekly in the *London Evening Standard*.

For the past 20 years she has divided her time between Dorset and County Roscommon in Ireland, where she co-founded the Strokestown International Poetry Festival, and of which she is Director. In 2002 she created the Dorset Big Cats Register with the aim of recording and publishing sightings of anomalous big cats in the county.

She has published five previous books, of which the best-selling *Mystery Big Cats* (2006) investigated the big cat phenomenon nationwide and received huge critical acclaim. She has given talks on the subject in the USA and England, and on BBC Radio 4.

In this book she turns her attention to her home county of Dorset, location of some of the closest and most vivid encounters with these elusive felines.

Seen something but not sure what it was? You're not alone! Log your sightings at Merrily's website – www.dorsetbigcats.org – or email research@dorsetbigcats.org.

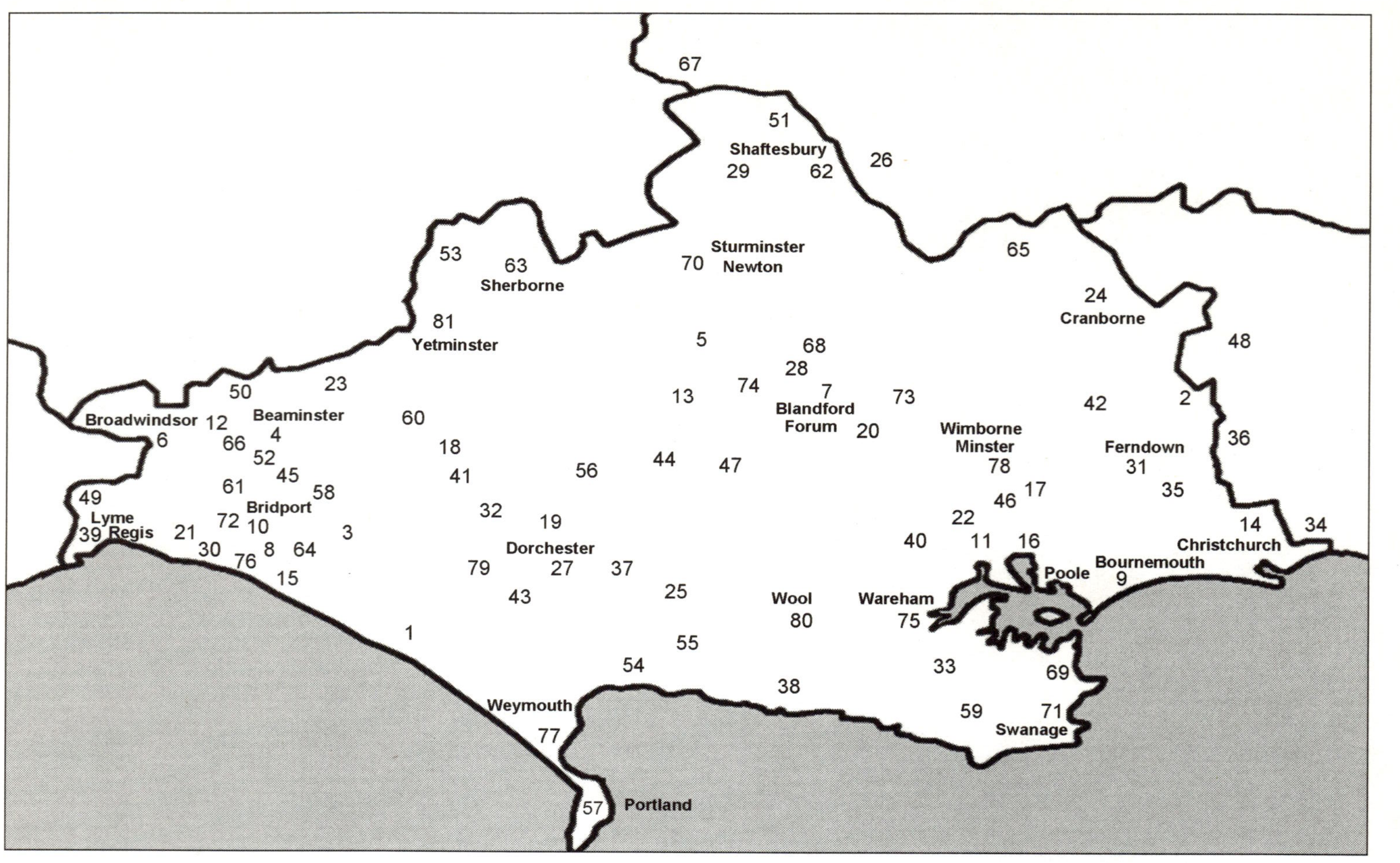

Broadwindsor
Lyme Regis
Beaminster
Bridport
Yetminster
Sherborne
Shaftesbury
Sturminster Newton
Cranborne
Blandford Forum
Wimborne Minster
Ferndown
Christchurch
Bournemouth
Poole
Wareham
Wool
Dorchester
Weymouth
Portland
Swanage

Areas Covered in the Gazetteer

Use the first numbers below to identify the locations on the map. The second bracketed numbers indicate the sighting count at each location when greater than one.

1 Abbotsbury (4)	22 Corfe Mullen	43 Martinstown	64 Shipton Gorge
2 Ashley Heath	23 Corscombe	44 Melcombe Bingham (2)	65 Sixpenny Handley (3)
3 Askerswell (3)	24 Cranborne (5)	45 Melplash (3)	66 Stoke Abbott (4)
4 Beaminster (4)	25 Crossways (6)	46 Merley	67 Stourhead (Wilts)
5 Belchalwell	26 Donhead St Mary (Wilts) (3)	47 Milton Abbas	68 Stourpaine
6 Birdsmoorgate	27 Dorchester (9)	48 Mockbeggar (Hants)	69 Studland (2)
7 Blandford (5)	28 Durweston (2)	49 Monkton Wyld	70 Sturminster Newton (4)
8 Bothenhampton (3)	29 East Stour (2)	50 Mosterton	71 Swanage
9 Bournemouth (3)	30 Eype (2)	51 Motcombe	72 Symondsbury (5)
10 Bridport (7)	31 Ferndown (4)	52 Netherbury (8)	73 Tarrant Rushton
11 Broadstone (2)	32 Frampton & Southover (3)	53 Nether Compton	74 Turnworth
12 Broadwindsor	33 Hartland Moor (2)	54 Osmington (2)	75 Wareham (10)
13 Bulbarrow Hill (2)	34 Hinton (Hants)	55 Owermoigne (2)	76 West Bay
14 Burton (Hants) (2)	35 Hurn, Airport (3)	56 Piddletrenthide (3)	77 Weymouth (10)
15 Burton Bradstock (6)	36 Kingston (Hants) (2)	57 Portland, Isle of (8)	78 Wimborne Minster (10)
16 Canford Heath (2)	37 Lower Bockhampton (2)	58 Powerstock (3)	79 Winterbourne Abbas
17 Canford Magna	38 Lulworth (5)	59 Purbeck, Isle of	80 Wool (3)
18 Cattistock	39 Lyme Regis (4)	60 Rampisham	81 Yetminster (2)
19 Charlton Down	40 Lytchett Matravers (2)	61 Salway Ash	
20 Charlton Marshall (2)	41 Maiden Newton (4)	62 Shaftesbury	
21 Chideock	42 Mannington	63 Sherborne (2)	

Introduction

Anomalous big cats – ABCs

The presence of anomalous big cats (ABCs for short) in our countryside is perhaps Britain's most intriguing mystery – and Dorset currently has the highest number of sightings per square mile than any other English county. These creatures first came to the notice of the media in the 1960s with sightings of big cats collectively known as the 'Surrey Puma', and in the 40 years since then, the annual number of sightings has increased hugely. It is now estimated to be running at somewhere between 1000 and 3000 a year countrywide.

It is an astonishing thing to see what is unmistakably a big cat in the British landscape – more so in the tranquil Dorset countryside. Kim Welsh, for instance, had just such an encounter near Kingston, Ringwood, on the Dorset/Hampshire border. On a bright morning in May 2001 she was driving her daughter home from a riding lesson. They had gone only about 250 yards out of the village, when they had an experience that Kim described as 'completely bizarre'. She said: 'We came round a slight bend to see a big, jet-black cat – the size of a panther – emerge from the left-hand-side hedge, and stop in the middle of the lane. I braked, but it didn't move so I then had to stop the car. It stood there only a few feet from the bonnet. The car is a Nissan Serena just over 5 ft 6 inches wide – and it was at least the whole width of the car. It had huge paws, a long tail looped up at the end, a panther-like domed head and amber eyes. It stayed completely still in front of the car looking at us for about 30 seconds, I should think, though it seemed like an eternity, and then it sauntered – with a typical feline gait – off to the right, and disappeared into the hedge. My daughter and I looked at each other in stunned silence; it was quite frightening, and I know it was silly but I locked the car door. You just don't see something like that.' Kim rang the police, and returned to the riding stables to warn them – they confirmed that other people had seen a similar animal.

One evening in June 2005 Sam Cooke went out to call his dog in, and found it staring tensely at the marsh at the bottom of a steep bank at the edge of his garden. 'She was looking towards the forest and seemed on edge', Sam recalled. 'I looked down the bank and saw bounding along the bottom what I at first thought was one of our neighbour's black Labradors – but then realised this was a slightly bigger animal with a much, much longer tail. It was about 25 m away, and running straight into the forest. It moved in a cat-like way – more elegant than a dog – but it was obviously not a

Sam Cooke and dog watched a black ABC running along the bottom of the hill

domestic cat. I was amazed. My dog was just sitting there looking at it as if amazed too.'

Two deer stalkers got within 50 yards of a black ABC on Bulbarrow Hill, and studied it though their telescopic rifle sights. One recorded the event in his diary: 'As we were walking uphill on the last 200 yards to the road, I saw my car and, rather oddly, a bulky item on the boot thereof. Who had dumped a bag on my boot, and for what reason? When we had approached to about a hundred yards of it, the 'bag' slowly unwound and languidly lowered its front feet to the ground – whilst the rear of the animal, for such it was, remained on the boot. A sizeable beast! I immediately chambered a round in my rifle, and looked at the apparition through my telescopic sights. By then it had all four feet on the ground, its eyes glinting with a faint yellowish tinge, and looked for all the world like a black panther. It was hard to believe that such an animal was there right in front of us, but my co-stalker and I agreed, with eyes firmly fixed on the cat, that that was the reason why we had seen no other animals during our evening. I was ready to shoot the beast if it approached us, but when we were at 50 yards from it, it turned and walked away slowly up the hill alongside my car, silhouetted on the horizon and no longer a safe shot, and into the woodland, out of sight. There was no doubt in our minds that we had seen a black big cat – a panther as far as I could judge.'

Thousands of people have this kind of experience every year, and in every county from Caithness to Cornwall and from Norfolk to Wales. In fact a glimpse of an ABC is now Britain's commonest brush with the unknown; probably more people see a mysterious big cat in the countryside each year than see a pig.

Mike and his co- deer stalker were this close to both the car and the panther

Reactions from other animals

Other animals spot them too, and their reactions confirm that ABCs are indeed exotic creatures to be reckoned with. The dogs of a police officer, Emma Hawkes, chased a puma-like ABC near Charlton Down on 13 July 2006: 'I was riding my horse at noon along a bridle path near the Old Sherborne Road, Dorchester. My two dogs were 50 m ahead of me when a large golden-brown-coloured animal, approximately 6 ft long and 2 ft 6 inches to 3 ft high, crossed the path in front of us – about 6 ft in front of the lead dog. It had a long sleek body with a thick tail as long as the body, and a rounded head. My bitch initially thought it was a deer and chased after it into a field of oil seed rape, but lost it. She returned a minute later and went off to her favourite pond for a swim as though nothing had happened. The horse wasn't spooked as we were too far away, and it (the cat) didn't seem at all interested in the dogs or the horse.'

Another witness described a confrontation between a deer and an ABC at Piddlehinton in September 2006, writing: 'I saw a big cat today. If you were to ask me what kind of cat it was I would have to say that it looked like a female lion or a young male lion. It sat watching me with its head above the grass. I was a long way from any habitation and I can tell you I was worried. Then I noticed a big stag in the corner of the field. The stag was also stood watching the animal. The stag came cautiously into the field and when the animal noticed it the stag charged at it. When the stag charged the animal I saw the full size of it. Although I was some distance away it was big, very big. It had a very big, long tail and it ran quickly in a leaping motion. Not like a dog … but huge and powerful.'

At 10.30 a.m. on 5 October 2004 Mr Batchelor was walking his lurcher in Wareham Forest. He had deliberately chosen a quiet part of the forest as his dog was in season. It was a quiet, clear and bright day. Suddenly he saw that his dog had seen something, as she was looking fixedly ahead and her hackles had risen and she was making quiet barks. Mr Batchelor said: 'She spots deer before I do, so I looked to see what it was. About 200 yards ahead, crossing the track, was a black, Labrador-sized, cat-like animal. It was just strolling. I don't think it was aware we were there. It had the typical, very long, curved tail – the classic thing – and its style of walking was definitive. I might have thought it was my imagination if it hadn't been for the dog seeing it first. It certainly stirred her up – and dogs haven't got any axe to grind have they?'

Perhaps the oddest association of animals, wild and domestic, was witnessed by Nick Pounder and his brother-in-law Jerry, in July 2002 on the road from Askerswell going towards Eggardon Hill: 'We were pottering slowly along, chatting, as it was a beautiful evening – when a domestic cat crossed the road about 10 yards in front of us'. To their surprise, this was followed a few seconds later, in the same place, by a fox, and then – amazingly – a badger. 'By then we had stopped to avoid running the animals over, and Jerry was just saying what a lot of wildlife there was about when his expression changed and he said "Look at that!" A coal-black cat at least as big as an Alsatian stepped out of the hedge in the same place and followed the procession across the road – we were just flabbergasted. It had a long, thin tail which curved to the ground and up again. We saw it go across the field towards Eggardon, but neither of us felt like getting out of the car!'

The road from Askerswell to Eggardon, where Nick Pounder and his brother-in-law witnessed an extraordinary procession of animals, including an ABC

Where have ABCs come from?

One theory regarding the origin of these cats is that they could have escaped from zoos or menageries in the past, and perhaps bred in the wild. Travelling menageries were certainly popular in the nineteenth century. The *Exeter Flying Post* of 1806 described one which visited Weymouth as displaying a Bengal tiger 'which devoured a whole bullock's head, horns and all', a lion and lioness, panthers, leopards, a hyena, a lynx, a kangaroo and an ostrich. Researcher Chris Moiser found records of the biggest menagerie, Wombwells, passing through Dorset in 1855, 1860, 1867 and 1868, stopping and exhibiting in Bridport, Weymouth, Dorchester, Blandford and Wimborne. However, numbers of travelling menageries dwindled at the outbreak of the First World War, and the last one went out of business in about 1931.

One drawback to the theory is that there is no evidence for it. Escapees are almost always easily recaptured, and those that are not immediately rounded up do not run off to live wild in the forest – even if there happens to be a handy forest nearby. On the contrary, they usually come back home for dinner by themselves. For instance in August 1975 an escaped leopard was easily caught when it obligingly wandered into a house in Fallowfield, Manchester. A pet puma escaped from a shed in Hampshire, and strolled aimlessly around the village gardens for a few hours before being recaptured.

In fact, of the 16 big cats known to have escaped into the wild in the UK between 1977 and 1998, 14 were recaptured within 24 hours, and the remaining two were shot.

Perhaps the most popular theory is that ABCs are simply the descendants of animals that were irresponsibly released from private collections when the Dangerous Wild Animals Act of 1976 made expensive licensing compulsory. This ignores the fact that there were many sightings of mysterious big cats before that date. Jim Miller, for instance, saw 'a bloody great cat' picking its way along White Nothe cliffs near Lulworth in the 1960s. 'It was black and near enough the size of a donkey in length but shorter legged, with a tail as long as its body.' He and his crew were in a fishing boat at the time and watched it for 20 minutes, clearly visible against the white cliffs, as it jumped two crevasses before disappearing over the cliff top.

There is much other evidence to suggest that ABCs are neither released pets nor escapees, nor the descendants of such hypothetical animals:

(1) The first body of evidence relates to the predominance of sightings of black ABCs. There are at present four species of big cats known to science – lions, tigers, leopards and their New World equivalent jaguars. An American puma, also called a cougar or mountain lion, is not *technically* a big cat, although it is the same size or bigger than a leopard, so for the purposes of this book I include it as one.

   The only big cat that has a black form is the leopard. Normally leopards have spotted coats, but occasionally one is born with black fur, and these animals are prized by zoos because they are rare. The popular term for a melanistic leopard (i.e. one that has been born with black fur) is a 'black panther' – and I use this term for a black leopard too.

   In the 1970s it was relatively cheap to buy a big cat. For instance, a zoo-bred lion cub or a puma could be bought for £20 (about £300 in today's money). However, black panthers were always rare and therefore expensive: in 1976, when the Dangerous Wild Animals Act came in, anyone who owned one could have sold it for £500, which was the cost of a small car, the equivalent of about £7000 today.

   There is no evidence that irresponsible owners did release big cats in any numbers – but it is reasonable to assume that if the owner of a menagerie *had* decided to offload some of his big cats, he would have released the cheaper, less dangerous, common pumas, or ordinary spotted leopards into the wild – while keeping the valuable black leopard to sell on. And yet, if the present 'sightings' statistics are anything to go by, he did the exact reverse.

   About 15% of sightings logged in the UK every year are of animals broadly resembling brown or fawn-coloured pumas, but 80% of sightings describe black panther-like animals.

   However, the really bizarre thing is that among the thousands of big cat sightings of the past 40 years, no witness has ever reported seeing a normal, spotted leopard.

(2) Given the huge number of sightings, it is a curious fact that none of these black panther-like animals has ever been caught – despite dozens of police hunts over the decades. The hunt for what became known as the Shooters Hill cheetah in east London was the biggest on record. Hundreds of people helped the police with tracker dogs, but to no avail. In recent years police hunts have called upon helicopters equipped with thermal imaging equipment; farmers have staged vigils; gun clubs

have staked out woodlands; and numerous people have set traps. Even the Marines spent months searching fruitlessly for the Beast of Exmoor – all without success.

Isn't it strange that our ABCs have escaped capture despite the same traps, lures, snares, farmers' and gamekeepers' guns, big game hunters, wildlife trackers, vigilantes and military operations that have made most big cats endangered species in their native lands? After 40 years of sightings there *should* be dozens of captured black panthers on display, alive and dead – not to mention regular road kills – but this has not happened.

(3) In addition to the bodies, there should be dozens of wildlife documentaries on ABCs, but so far there is not even a really clear photo of one. There are various snippets of film footage and photos which are certainly suggestive of big cats, but nothing detailed enough to establish what species they might be. One of the best was taken by Tara-Leigh Eggiman and two colleagues who saw an ABC at Burton Bradstock in November 2006. They were about 200 yards away and estimated it was about 3 ft long, excluding the tail. Despite the obviously feline quality of the animal in the image it is impossible to gather enough detail to identify it more accurately. Photos like these almost constitute proof – but not quite. But then ABC research is the science of almost.

An ABC near Burton Bradstock. (Photo credit: Tara-Leigh Eggiman)

(4) There is also the ubiquity of the phenomenon. From John O' Groats to Land's End, the same range of black, panther-like animals, brown puma-like or lynx-like felines are reported. There have even been four or five reliable sightings of black ABCs on the Isle of Mull over a 30-year period.

This puts the final nail in the coffin of the releases and escapes theories, because Mull has never had any zoos, or private menageries, and it is half an hour by boat from the mainland, so you would need to be mad to convey a leopard there. And you would have to be even madder to do it at least twice, since leopards live for only 15 years at the most.

(5) Finally, there are the puzzling variations in the colours, shapes and sizes of ABCs, according to eyewitness reports. They are variously described as being the size of a Labrador, German shepherd, collie, whippet or Great Dane dog, a fox, a sheep, a calf, a goat, a deer – even 'a small horse.'

When they are not plain, glossy black, ABCs' colours are equally variable: they have been described as grey, white, tawny, dark brown, beige, brindled, black-tailed, chocolate and many more colour variations. Sometimes brown animals have ringed tails or lighter patches. They may have amber, or yellow, or green glowing eyes, or red or blue eyes.

The commonest kind of ABCs – the jet black animals – may also have brown patches or white tips to their tails, or tufted or pointed ears, and so on. Lynx-like creatures, distinguished by their long, black ear-tufts, may also have long tails – a feature that rules out the conventional European or Siberian lynxes which have short tails – stumps almost – no more than about 6 inches long. The ABC one witness encountered near Cattistock (perhaps well-named!), and accurately described, was just such a creature:

'In the autumn of 1986 I was walking with my baby in a pram on the road going from Maiden Newton to Cattistock, and had neared Cattistock, going past a stretch of land that kept chickens on at the time. I saw what seemed to be a lynx. It was only a few feet away from me and walked quite slowly and stealthily across the field in front of me. Its appearance was tabby cat – but the size of a large Labrador with very upright pointed ears with long upright dark tufts. It looked right at me with a glare, very bright eyes. It held my gaze all the way across the field in front of me. The tail was bushy and long with dark stripes or rings, and dark at the tip (like a racoon's tail markings). I had a very good view of it as it was so close to me and I didn't even think to be frightened!'

Or what are we to make of the animal that confused two women near Wynford Eagle in March 2007? Virginia Astley and Catherine Simmonds had gone for a walk on the old railway line to Toller Fratrum. Virginia recalled: 'We were coming from Wynford Eagle to Maiden Newton, and half way along on the left-hand side there is a barn. We saw an animal – the top of it, then it vanished. The thought that it could be a deer or fox obviously crossed our minds, and Catherine has always lived in the country and is familiar with these animals. Then we saw it completely, going towards a gate. It was bizarre; a very orangey colour, too big for a domestic cat – a big dog size. It looked like a kind of toy, so completely not like anything I'd ever seen – a small orange lion. It was in a field with a stream to the left, on the far side of the stream, about a hundred metres away, walking along parallel with us. It then vanished out of view and a rabbit came tearing across the field towards us. I didn't notice much of a tail. It had a strange shaped head, quite fluffyish. Just wasn't like anything. We were so mystified and wondered if it was some kind of odd pet. The colour was almost unreal. If either of us had been alone we would have thought we had imagined it.'

The oddities of appearance which distinguish ABCs from known species of big cats constitute an enduring headache for those ABC investigators trying to pigeonhole them. The zoologist Dr Karl Shuker put it succinctly: 'The British big cat would need to be nothing short of a shape-shifter to account for the immense variety of felids reported.'

Where do ABCs go?

However, if these inconsistencies are puzzling, there is worse to come. ABCs not only resist capture, apparently disappearing off the face of the earth, but they sometimes disappear actually in front of people's eyes.

The naturalist Jonathan McGowan and a group of friends had crossed a small bridge onto an island in the River Stour in Dorset, when they surprised a puma-like creature drinking at the river's edge. He warned the others to keep back as the animal dashed for the escape route over the wooden walkway – but then it disappeared before their amazed eyes. Jonathan ran forward in disbelief to find one wet paw print fading on the planks.

Trevor Beer, a Devon writer and big cat investigator, also noted the phenomenon. 'Many is the time I and others have watched such a cat crossing an open hillside when it has "vanished" as if into thin air, presumably into a cave or some hidden goyal as we locals call the smaller coombes or unfarmed bits of countryside hereabouts. Yet, as often as not, on going to what seems the exact spot, we find that the animal has disappeared, with the terrain showing no obvious hiding places.

At such moments the air feels charged with electricity as one's own "hackles" rise at the back of the neck and one feels as if one is in the presence of unseen, watching eyes, which is probably the case. Once two of us watched a black leopard coming towards us along a disused green lane, from a vantage point looking down along its length. The lane was bordered with trees and bushes with steepish fields on either side and leading to a waterway below. The cat came to a gorse patch, but instead of appearing out of the other side it vanished. I say "vanished" because though it might simply have lain down to rest up amongst the gorse, when we went down to look, it had gone. Yet I feel sure that at no time as we walked down to the lane did I lose sight of the spot' (taken from Trevor Beer's book, *The Beast of Exmoor: Fact or Legend?*)

Adrian Carson was fishing on the River Lugar in Ayrshire, Scotland, when he came round a bend and there in front of him, he said, 'as plain as day' was a large, black, panther-like cat – standing there looking at him. 'I was rooted to the spot with fear at first, but slowly started to walk backwards. I stumbled on a log and took my eyes off the animal for a spilt-second, and when I looked up it had vanished.'

However, disappearing into thin air is only one of the habits of ABCs that distinguish them from their zoological counterparts. They also have the habit of moving occasionally with 'incredible speed', unlike the leopards of television documentaries which are not habitual runners and rely mainly on ambush to capture their prey. At other times they move with surreal slowness – 'it just strolled across the road, completely unconcerned' is an oft repeated mantra among eyewitnesses. The cats sometimes glance at the witness, or stare, but often they seem indifferent, moving dreamily in a world of their own, only to melt into the hedge or over the brow of a hill never to reappear.

Roars, growls and screams

Moreover, the various sounds ABCs make do not fit exactly with their zoological counterparts either. One of the definitions of a big cat is that it can roar. Lions, tigers, jaguars and leopards can all roar, while the puma and lynx are technically classed as small cats because they cannot.

This is because of differences in the hyoid bone which connects the tongue to the roof of the mouth. In big cats this has an elastic segment, while that of small cats is hard all over. It is this that allows big cats to produce a roar, and which also prevents them from purring in the manner of the small cats. All cats can snarl and growl; pumas are also capable of whistles, purrs and moans. However, their unique and distinctive sound is the blood-curdling screaming, yowling or caterwauling by which female pumas signal their readiness to mate.

ABCs are also apparently capable of a wide range of sounds, from deafening roars to threatening hisses; but perhaps the sounds most commonly associated with ABCs are screaming or yowling, very like – so earwitnesses say – those of a puma.

Michael Davis of Bridport both saw and heard an ABC. It was exactly 5 o'clock on the morning of 25 August 2002 when he and his wife were awakened by a spine-chilling noise. 'It was like a screech owl, dog, cat all put together.' They decided not to investigate it, but the following morning – 'curiously enough', said Mr Davis, 'it was at exactly 5 o'clock again' – they heard it once more. This time they got up and looked outside. Sitting on the low wall directly below their bedroom window they saw a large black cat of about 4 ft in length, with a long tail, and teeth which were showing white. 'It sat on the wall next to our garden for about 10 minutes, but when we opened the window it bounded off.'

In the case of Chris Austin, his wife and friends, Mr and Mrs Hayes, it was an eerie shriek which first drew their attention to what they described as 'a total surprise'. Chris recalled: 'We were out rambling at the time, and had stopped to look at the distant view of Corfe Castle from the unusual angle that the walk presented, and saying wasn't it wonderful. Suddenly we heard a high shrieking noise, and looked at each other as if to say what's that? A bank rises from the side of the path, and we looked up this gradient and saw two cats about 30 yards away in one of the trees on the skyline. One of them moved – at which the branch broke and he fell 4 or 5 ft to the ground. The other one was higher up the tree and also climbed down, and they both made off. We ran up to the top of the slope – but they had gone.'

The group studied the rotten branch and Mrs Hayes photographed a paw print left at the foot of the tree. She was shocked by the incident – 'I was rooted to the spot – I just didn't believe it. We weren't frightened as it was so amazing we didn't have time to think about it.' The group agreed that the strange felines 'were not as big as an Alsatian – about Labrador-sized but with very long tails curled up at the end. One cat was very black and the other was slightly browny-black.'

All these felines were making the noise usually attributed to pumas; yet they were black – and pumas are never black.

Classifying ABCs

Everyone who attempts to classify ABCs finds that the more research they do into them the more insistent their oddities become – until he or she is forced to concede defeat. In fact you could say that the only characteristic common to all ABCs is that they more or less resist classification. In this respect they have much in common with the hundreds of other unnerving, annoying, entrancing beings that have likewise infested our landscape from time immemorial: the 'black dogs' of legend and folklore; fairies, boggarts, pixies, lake monsters, brownies, 'white ladies', water-horses and so on – there are hundreds of varieties. Like ABCs they are elusive by definition; like them, too, they appear sometimes bigger than normal, and sometimes smaller; like them they are ambiguous.

There are places in the Dorset landscape where encounters with anomalous felines seem to be part of this older tradition. The earliest record of a big cat in Dorset comes from a 1907 manuscript entitled *Reminiscences of Sturminster Newton*, by Robin Young, and quoted in *Dark Dorset* by R.J. Newland and M.J. North. Young was a Sturminster man, looking back to his schooldays in the 1820s. He remarked that teachers should 'not allow absurd stories to be told before timid and sensitive children'. For example: 'A story was often told them of a wild and savage cat which haunted the remains of the old castle and was often seen on Newton Hill. Such horrid tales were told of this monster cat, with eyes as big as tea saucers that many children were afraid to pass that way, and not only children but grown-up people would be so afraid that they would walk on the main road below the hill to avoid the creature. I am pleased to know that foolish tale is quite forgotten'.

The folklorist Jeremy Harte writes: 'On the Island of Purbeck, in my native Dorset, the old road used to pass through a toll gate just outside Ulwell, and a cottage beside the road was home to the witch Jinny Gould. She used to sit out on the gate at nights in the form of a cat, getting a lot of fun out of terrifying travellers, until one drunken carter picked up enough daring to land her a blow across the back with his whip. Suddenly the cat vanished, and back in the cottage Jinny lay dead (Luckham 1906). Today both the toll gate and the cottage are gone, although haunted gates survive elsewhere in the county. Normally it is ghosts which sit on these liminal markers' (*At the Edge* No.6, 1997).

Liminal markers are boundaries between places, both natural and manmade, such as streams, bridges, walls, crossroads and gateways. Traditionally such places are portals through which this world and the daimons' otherworld can meet. For instance the black ABC that Anne Coombs saw at Bruton in Somerset passed through an archway into the churchyard (October 1995).

The Cathole area between Shipton Gorge and Burton Bradstock is steeped in folklore. Local stories tell of otherworldly encounters on misty nights. Rodney Legg wrote in *Mysterious Dorset* (p.19): 'A phantom dog is said to cross Bredy Lane. Mrs Muriel Aylott who lived in Shipton Gorge in the 1920s told me in 1969: "It's said that he came from a ditch, passed over from one side of the road and went into a hollow or ditch on the other side. But I don't know anything more than that". The dog is said to cross the lane between Cathole Copse and Cathole Barn – Cattle the locals call it – which is about 300 yards north of Bredylane Cottage.' Or was it a big cat as the local place names suggest?

A short distance west lies the parish boundary at St Catherine's Cross – another classic liminal marker – and here, according to Rodney Legg, on some nights there is seen a spectral coach and horses, accompanied by a headless black dog. It was at this spot that in 1999 a cyclist, Stuart, had an odd experience. He wrote: 'It would have been late afternoon with the sun very low in the sky. I was cycling west along Bennetts Hill Lane when I noticed a disturbance in a group of cows further down the hill. For a moment I thought I saw a black animal moving fast about 20 ft from the cows, but I had sweat in my eyes which I wiped away. When I looked again the animal was not visible.' Perhaps the cows were aware of an invisible presence, for he noted, 'they were clearly still excited … they seemed panicky and unsure of where to run'.

St Catherine's cross, the site of Stuart's sighting, or near it – an example of a liminal place

While these examples seem to connect ABCs with liminal places, ABCs are far more likely to have a connection with certain topographical features of the landscape. Research (comprehensively reviewed in my previous book, *Mysterious Big Cats*) suggests that, for instance, a disproportionate number of ABC sightings in Britain are made close to or on railway lines, used and disused. They are also apt to appear near quarries, tunnels, steep hillsides and hollows.

Do these patterns suggest that there is something inherent in the landscape that favours the appearances of ABCs in these locations? The Chinese believe that the confluence and divergence of complementary earth energies – personified as the white tiger and the azure dragon – can create conditions conducive to the manifestation of otherworldly beings: an idea familiar to the West as an element of *Feng Shui*. As Ernest J. Eitel put it: 'Nature's breath contains a twofold element, a male and female, positive and negative, expanding and reverting breath, resembling as we in modern English would put it, two magnetic currents, or, as the Chinese put it, the azure dragon and the white tiger. Where there is a true dragon, there will also be a tiger, and the two will be traceable in the outlines of mountains or hills running in a tortuous and curved course' (*Feng Shui: The Science of Sacred Landscape in Old China*).

Could there be something about Dorset's confluence of small, steep hills and the long ribbons of railway line that favour the appearance of ABCs, as traditional cultures might believe? Spencer Allen's ABC, for instance, appeared in just such a geomantically suggestive landscape near Dorchester. He recalled: 'There are water meadows on the right, divided from a steep hill by a railway track running parallel to the road. I saw a black cat-like animal with a very long tail running diagonally down the hill towards the railway line. I slowed down and watched it for about 10 seconds. At that moment a train came along, going the other way. Its size enabled me to gauge the size of the cat, and I thought "God, that was big!" I estimated it as just over a metre with a smooth tail of about 70 cm, curving down and up again in an S shape. The train obscured my view of the cat, and when it had passed the cat had gone.'

There is no ready answer to these questions, but while the puzzle of ABC appearances remains so baffling it is as well not to exclude any theory.

It is not only ABCs that have something mysterious about them: our own domestic moggies are implicated in many ABC sightings. Nick Pounder's procession of animals, for instance, began with a small domestic cat and culminated in an ABC. Jeremy Harte has noted that our pet cats are ambiguous, intermediate creatures, forming a bridge between the human and animal worlds – between the indoor world of the warm fireside and the nocturnal wilderness, coming and going between the two with equal purposefulness. In folklore the domestic cat acts also as an intermediary between this world and the Otherworld. Pure black cats have always been witches' familiars, and sometimes, like Jinny Gould's cat, interchangeable with the witch herself. As a Galway man said: 'Some ways they would put a dread on you. What company do they keep? When the moon is riding high and the wind tearing the trees, and the shadows black with cold, who is it calls them from the hearth? Tell me that.' (Henry Glassie, *Irish Folk-Tales*, p.178)

What are ABCs?

The greatest authorities on such intermediate beings were the Neoplatonists who flourished in Ancient Greece from about the middle of the third century A.D. to the middle of the sixth. They called them *daimones* (pronounced *die-moan-ays*) – or as we would say, daimons (N.B. *not* 'demons' but pronounced *day-mons*). According to those philosophers the domain of the daimons was the *Anima Mundi*, the Soul of the World, a middle region in a chain of existence between the One – the transcendent source of all things – and the quotidian materiality of human life. In this way they partook of both kinds of reality – they were both material and immaterial.

However, the Greek notion of intermediate beings is thoroughly unpopular nowadays. We simply cannot get our heads round the idea that something may be absolutely concrete, but only temporarily so; absolutely real, but not in scientifically repeatable terms. We are too literal-minded, preferring things to be black or white, while the world of daimons is crepuscular, glimpsed out of the corner of the eye, resistant to being caught and pigeon-holed.

Nevertheless, there is much to suggest that ABCs are daimons, and, moreover, daimons uniquely tailored to our age and culture – an age and culture that does not believe in them. For in order not to be ignored they have had to assume a form that positively demands attention – the terrifyingly solid, glossy black 'predator'. And compared to the wary and modest daimons of earlier times they are unusually insistent – they stroll around in broad daylight, they eat sheep, they chase deer, they roar, they scream, they stop cars, they jump out in front of cyclists, they astonish Sunday afternoon strollers.

Because, the fact is that the modern ABC experience is about as vivid, concrete and un-ghostlike as it gets. People who have had such an encounter are all agreed about that, and it is on such first-hand accounts that the reality of ABCs ultimately depends. To illustrate this point let me quote two of the most interesting and dramatic encounters with big cats on record. They happened to Dorset people – and, like most ABC witnesses, typically pleasant, sensible, solid and sober citizens.

In March 2004 shepherd Steve Evans noticed that sheep were disappearing from the farm where he worked, just south of Beaminster, and he had been finding their remains. On Saturday 6 March he had found a large sheep, skinned and with quite a lot of meat missing, but the skeleton intact. Two days later – a clear, still, silent day – he was riding a quad bike along a track that looks down into a small, deep valley when he thought he saw a black dog. He said: 'I saw what I thought at first was a Labrador, then another one appeared, and I realised they were more like cats. I stalled the quad and sat there watching them from about 200 yards away, but above them, as they circled a patch of brambles, as though they were after a rabbit in it or something'. Then to his surprise a larger cat-like animal appeared. This one was bigger, about the height of an Alsatian, but longer. 'She just appeared out of nowhere and stood there watching them. She was black and glossy as though the coat was shining'. He reckons it was a mother and two cubs. The animals had distinctive long, swooping tails that curled up at the end. They were jet shiny black with no markings. He watched them for around 15 minutes before coasting down towards them on the bike, with the engine off, but he had to take a circuitous route behind a hedgerow, and by the time he reached the bottom of the coombe they had gone. However, they had left behind a strong, pungent odour of a kind he did not recognise. 'Not like a fox. I've never smelt anything like it before'.

This was not the first time Steve had seen a big cat in the vicinity. About 2 years previously, when a neighbouring shoot was in progress, he had observed a large, black panther-like animal making its way down the side of a hill and disappearing into cover. He had been reluctant to believe the evidence of his own eyes, but the sighting was later confirmed

Steve Evans watched an Alsatian-sized big cat and two Labrador-sized cubs playing in a valley near Beaminster

by several of the guns who had also spotted it.

Karen Rees ordinarily goes for a walk on Askers Meadow, near Bridport, every morning at 5.30 a.m. with her dog, Sunny, a large, black Labrador lurcher cross. She told me: 'I usually meet my Mum there who also has a black Labrador, Mia. Hers is very, very glossy because my Dad used to be a Metropolitan police dog-handler and buffs Mia up with chamois leather. We usually circle a long, thicket-style hedge between two meadows – she goes one way and I go the other and we meet the far side of the thicket. The morning of Friday 11 July 2003 was a beautiful morning and I was marvelling at it – everything was very still – and thinking vaguely about the day's work ahead. Then, about 30 yards away, just behind the barbed wire fence at the edge of the thicket I saw what I thought was Mum's dog, lying injured – a hind leg with a really glossy black coat. I went towards it thinking, "Oh God – that's Mia", but as I got closer I realised it was much too big to be Mia. It was lying completely motionless, but when I was within a few feet of it and just beginning to call "Mia", it sprang up. It went from lying down to all four paws in the blink of an eye! I didn't see it get to its feet – it was lying down one moment and the next it wasn't. I was near enough to have touched it. As it sprang up it bared its teeth at me and made a peculiar half hissing, half growling, guttural noise which I took to mean "bugger off and leave me alone". (I was more than happy to oblige!)

The two things that most affected me were its eyes and teeth. I saw that the canines were about 2 to 3 inches long. Its eyes were a smoky amber colour – as if an orange had a grey veil over it, or, although it sounds clichéd, the same colour as the light vein of a piece of polished Tiger's Eye gem stone. It made a blood-curdling noise – neither a hiss nor a growl, but a very guttural noise, difficult to describe. It then turned and made off into the thicket, and I estimated its size as being three times the size of Sunny, not including the tail – and not including Sunny's tail. The tail was very long and hooked up at the end. Sunny had not seen the cat at he was chasing rabbits some distance away, but when he got back to me he stayed very close beside me, which is most uncharacteristic of him, because he is the kind of dog who runs energetically about. When I got to the stile at the other side of the thicket I saw my Mum coming towards me with Mia, and looked about to see if I could see where the cat had gone. I just caught sight of its backside and tail disappearing into a hedge running at right angles to the original thicket, about 50 yards away. I told my mother what I had seen, but she had not spotted the animal as she walked round her side of the thicket.' Karen rang the police when she got home, but their subsequent search failed to find the animal.

Karen went home and, needless to say, reported the alarming event to the police who immediately searched the area. But it seemed that, just like the daimonic beings of former times, the animal had simply turned tail and vanished – for the police failed to find it or anything resembling it.

With so much evidence proving them to be preternaturally elusive creatures, it is difficult to resist the idea that ABCs might somehow equate to the daimons of old, but in new guises – as black or golden big cats.

Conclusion

There is nothing definite about ABCs except the absolute reality of experiences such as those I have described above, and the many others that follow in the gazetteer section of this book. Of course this is also the joy of ABCs: they are easily the most superb mystery available today, mediating – in true daimon style – between the worlds of reason and imagination. Our job is perhaps simply to notice them, and marvel at them, as many ABC witnesses do. One thing is certain, though – we deny them at our peril. Because, as the philosopher Plutarch reminds us: 'He who denies the daimons breaks the chain that unites the world to God.'

Karen's encounter – as inexplicable as it was closely observed – illustrates more vividly than most the nature of the daimonic world: it is just the other side of the metaphorical fence – and a flimsy wire fence at that – appearing and disappearing in, as she put it, 'the blink of an eye'.

The sight of an ABC brings about a change of perspective; it restores a world view where landscape is the imaginative matrix from which we all derive our sense of mystery and meaning, and reveals Dorset to be just as mysterious as any African rain forest.

Paw print comparisons

Gazetteer of Big Cat Sightings and Encounters

The following sightings are grouped under main place name headings, with exact locations (if supplied) and approximate date of the encounter. If you are looking for a particular place, search A to Z initially; if you don't find what you're looking for, then see the map at the beginning of the book and look up the nearest large town or village. Also refer to the index at the back of the book which lists all the places mentioned in the text.

Abbotsbury

12 February 1997

The *Dorset Echo* stated: 'There have been several reported sightings of a black, cat-like creature prowling around the village. One eye-witness is shepherd Stewart Pullen who saw the creature early one morning when he was feeding his flock. "At first I thought 'whose dog is that?' I got a bit closer and saw it stalking like a cat. When it saw me it got up and ran. It jumped through the fence. There is no way it was a dog – the speed it was going – and it had a very long, black tail."'

2002

A black big cat was reportedly seen running across a field above the beach.

Swannery and Clayhanger Farm – Summer 2005

There were two sightings of black, panther-like big cats between Abbotsbury Swannery and Clayhanger Farm on the Rodden Road on separate days, but within a few hundred yards of each other, in the early summer of 2005. The witness, Richard, wrote: 'The first sighting was a quick flash as I and a passenger were driving past a recently ploughed but very dry field. We both saw a black cat about a hundred yards away on our right-hand side, just before it was obscured by a hedge. We stopped, reversed, had another look but it had vanished through the hedge on the opposite side of the field. We drove up the road to a gateway, jumped out and went into the field, but we could not see it in the next field. We both agreed that it was black, had a long tail which was larger at the end and its size was bigger than a dog fox. I didn't bother to look for tracks as the soil was baked hard in the sun.

The second sighting was while I was on the same road but a couple of months later. I was driving down hill, on my own, and I saw a black cat bounding across a green field on my right. I stopped and watched it for a few seconds before it reached a hedge and stopped. It turned round – no it didn't – it turned its head and looked in my general direction. It was at this point about 150 yards away. It was swishing its tail and seemed to be just enjoying the sunshine! Then it bounded/jumped into the hedge and was gone. I waited as the field the other side of the hedge rose sharply to a high ridge. I got out my field glasses, but it did not reappear. I assume that it was following the line of the hedge. I would have stayed watching, but it is a single track road and a car came up behind me so I had to move.

The coast road to Abbotsbury

27 January 2007

A walker wrote: 'I often walk around Abbotsbury and recently came across a large paw print with no claw marks. I have a photo of this using a cigarette packet as a scale … . The tracks seemed fresh (broke away easily when touched) and there seemed to be a silence in the area.'

🐾 Ashley Heath

Moors Valley Golf Course – April 2005

A friend of a witness reported: 'A friend at work who often plays golf at Moors Valley Country Park informed me that some golfers ahead of her on the course had rushed back and said they were going back because they had seen a large brown cat. My friend continued slowly and looking in the bunker saw a paw print larger than her hand – and up ahead was a large, light brown cat staring at them. After a minute or two it continued into the forest and was not seen again.'

🐾 Askerswell

July 2002

A woman and her friend spotted 'a sleek, jet-black, cat-like creature about 2 ft long with a very long tail that curved round'. According to the *Dorset Echo* (20 Sept 2002) the beast had been spotted nearby at the same time the previous year.

Eggardon – July 2002

Nick Pounder had an extraordinary experience which definitively established the size of at least one Dorset big cat – he could compare it with three other species. He was driving along a lane near Askerswell with his brother-in-law Jerry and 'we were pottering slowly along, chatting, as it was a beautiful evening, when a domestic cat crossed the road about 10 yards in front of us'. To their surprise, this was followed a few seconds later, in the same place, by a fox, and then – amazingly – a badger. 'By then we had stopped to avoid running the animals over, and Jerry was just saying what a lot of wildlife there was about when his expression changed and he said "Look at that!" A coal-black cat at least as big as an Alsatian stepped out of the hedge in the same place and followed the procession across the road – we were just flabbergasted.'

Nick thought the panther was aware of them as it seemed to turn its back on them slightly and head more away from the car rather than directly after the other animals. He remembers seeing the back end of the animal as it melted into the undergrowth. 'It had a long, thin tail which curved to the ground and up again. We saw it go across the field towards Eggardon, but neither of us felt like getting out of the car!'

Chilcombe Hill – 20 October 2007

Rob and Ellen Roberts were walking their dog at Chilcombe Hill when they spotted a big cat: 'It came through a hedge about a hundred yards away, looked at us and the dog, then turned and walked away. It was black and about half as big again as our black Labrador; its ears I think were rounded, and its tail was long and sweeping down.'

🐾 Beaminster

Farm, south of Beaminster – 8 March 2004

Shepherd Steve Evans had a remarkable sighting of three panther-like animals on his farm just south of Beaminster. He'd noticed that he was losing sheep and had been finding their remains. On Saturday 6 March he had found a large sheep, skinned and with quite a lot of meat missing, but the skeleton intact. Two days later – a clear, still, silent day – he was riding a quad bike along a track that looks down into a small, deep valley when he thought he saw a black dog. He reported: 'I saw what I thought at first was a Lab, then another one appeared, and I realised they were more like cats. I stalled the quad and sat there watching them from about 200 yards away, but above them, as they circled a patch of brambles, as though they were after a rabbit in it or something'. Then to his surprise a larger cat-like animal appeared. This one was bigger, about the height of an Alsatian, but longer. 'She just appeared out of nowhere and stood there watching them. She was black and glossy as though the coat was shining'. He reckons it was a mother and two cubs. The animals had distinctive long, swooping tails that curled up at the end. They were jet, shiny black with no markings. He watched them for around 15 minutes before coasting down towards them on the bike, with the engine off, but he had to take a circuitous route behind a hedgerow, and by the time he reached the bottom of the coombe they had gone. However, they had left behind a strong, pungent odour of a kind he did not recognise. 'Not like a fox. I've never smelt anything like it before.'

'Bunny Valley' on a farm near Beaminster. Steve Evans saw a family of ABCs playing in front of the gorse bush on the right

This was not the first time Steve had seen a big cat in the vicinity. About 2 years previously, when a neighbouring shoot was in progress, he had observed a large, black panther-like animal making its way down the side of a hill and disappearing into cover. He had been reluctant to believe the evidence of his own eyes, but the sighting was later confirmed by several of the guns who had also spotted it.

Broadwindsor Road – August 2004

In August 2004, Simon Beal was driving back from Beaminster on the B3163 Broadwindsor road when he spotted something very similar to the animal he had seen from Melplash in 1995. It was early evening and bright and sunny. He had passed an industrial estate, and had just rounded a corner when, about a hundred yards ahead of him, he saw the back end of an animal with a very long tail disappearing into the hedge. It was dark brown or black, and about the size of an Alsatian dog. He stopped and looked into the field beyond the hedge but could not get another look at it.

Horn Hill House – 23 June 2006

The *Bridport News* reported: 'A mysterious big cat has again been sighted on the prowl in West Dorset. Beaminster couple Ken and Vera Caldwell spotted a tiger-like beast twice in just a few days. They first saw the animal through their kitchen window on a clear sunny morning last week at around 6 a.m. Mr Caldwell, of Horn Hill House, said: "It was slowly walking along the edge of the lawn about 30 m distant. At first we thought it was a large fox, but we soon realised that the colour, face and the tail were wrong. I watched it through binoculars and saw that the colour was a sandy colour, lighter than a fox; its side was marked with vertical broken stripes of darker fawn colour, exactly like a tiger. Its tail was almost as long as its body and very bushy, the same colour as the body. As he was walking along, his face appeared quite flat; then he became aware that he was under observation, he stopped and stared at us for a few seconds. Through the binoculars his face was wide and squarish with short ears and markings exactly like a tiger."

A few days later they saw what appeared to be the same animal lying on the lawn in between patches of rough about 40 m away. Mr Caldwell added: "The time was about 5.45 a.m. and my wife first observed it through the bathroom window, and she thought it was a deer, but soon decided it was different. My wife came downstairs to get the binoculars, but could not see him because of a dip in the ground. She opened the kitchen door quietly and was able to watch him for about 15 seconds. The animal was aware of being observed, he stared back for about 10–15 seconds, then stood up and ambled across the garden and down the driveway until he disappeared round the bend."

Mr Caldwell says he has now warned all his family not to disturb the animal and is hoping to capture the beast on video or a camera. He said: "We watched it walk about 100 yards up the path and as it went past the window we thought it was a funny looking fox, then it got closer and no way it was a fox, but the length of its tail was just amazing and it was bushy like a fox but at the end was a big black blob. It was a cat, there's no doubt whatsoever it was a cat. It stopped and faced me and it was only about 30 m from me and I had a pair of binoculars on it and it was a tiger. There's no doubt about it. All we can do is hope it comes again and we can get a picture of it."'

Tunnel Road – 5 February 2008

The *Dorset Echo* reported: 'Pensioner Gwen Wragg from Beaminster swears she was stone cold sober when she saw a black panther-like creature cavorting about her garden. Mrs Wragg, 84, of Tunnel Road, saw the creature around lunchtime and watched it in her garden for at least 5 minutes. She said: "It had to be a cat. It was a great big puma-like thing. I was looking out of the sun lounge at the top of my garden where I have a bed of cat mint which normal cats love. It was slowly bobbing up and down and when it very slowly turned around I could see it had a long black bushy tail and then it turned around and jumped up out of the bed towards my herbaceous border and pounced on something."

The sighting of a big cat is the most recent of a series in west and north Dorset. Mrs Wragg said the cat was very large and not a domestic pet. "It was very, very big and making its way down my herbaceous border and then started to scrape a swathe of earth up", she said. "I watched it for a while and then thought: Enough is enough. It is going to destroy my garden. I went towards the back door which is glass and continued to watch it. It was like no cat I had ever seen. The moment I opened the door it stopped and looked at me. It had a broad, chunky face and I would swear it had yellow eyes and very sharp, up-pointed ears. Then it turned into the border and jumped over the stone wall. I went to look at the swathe it had been raking up and it was 4–5 inches wide and no pussy could have made it. I was not frightened I was just entranced; I couldn't believe what I was looking at. I was stone cold sober, I swear.'"

🐾 Belchalwell

October 2001
Police reports show a big cat was observed by a shocked witness. It was described as creamy beige, with tiny pointed ears.

🐾 Birdsmoorgate

Pilsden Pen – July 2002
A witness reported: 'I was driving home on a July evening in 2002 at about 9 p.m., along the Marshwood to Broadwindsor road. At the area between Birdsmoorgate and Pilsden Hill a yellowy-brown big cat ran out into the road in front of me, between my car and the car in front. I have lived in the country all my life and am certain it was not a deer, dog, fox or anything like that. It was definitely a cat, and the long rounded tail, arched up, distinguished it beyond doubt. It was about 4–6 ft long and 2–3 ft high. It ran bounding across the road with a fluid movement, and through the hedge. I didn't mention it to anyone at first in case they thought I must be mad, but I have heard subsequently of other people seeing it around. I was talking to a gamekeeper who had something similar in his sights, but was too unnerved to shoot.'

🐾 Blandford

Blandford, Shillingstone and Longham Bridge – 1980s
The *Dorset Echo*, 4 March 2002, reported: 'The Chairman of the Bournemouth Natural History Society's zoology section, Jonathan McGowan, saw a puma stalking a badger near Blandford in the 1980s. "I thought, this cannot be true, they don't exist here. But I watched it for about half an hour." He also saw a female big cat in season walking around in circles calling for a mate like a domestic cat.

Later the same year he was watching a buzzard nest near Shillingstone when he noticed a big hole in a chalk quarry. There were deer leg bones outside. He said it didn't look like a fox earth … . However, on a subsequent visit he said he spotted two little heads. "They looked very cat-like," he said. His suspicion was confirmed when he saw a puma he presumed was the mother walking around the bottom of the quarry. "I realised then it was obviously the lair of the cats and the two heads I saw were cubs." Three years later he saw a puma drinking from the River Stour by Longham Bridge and he says he has seen scratches on trees and smelt smells not consistent with local wildlife.'

Bryanston – June 2001

Several witnesses reported a large, black cat-like animal in the vicinity.

Bryanston School – 8 July 2004

A large panther-like cat was spotted at 3 p.m. in the area of Bryanston School.

June 2005

A witness wrote: 'We were staying in Dorset in June 2005 in a campsite surrounded by woodland near Blandford Forum. My family and I had all gathered in Blandford for a funeral at the garrison in Blandford and as there were rather a lot of us we were all camping nearby. On the afternoon of the 23rd we decided to go for a walk in the woods. Everyone else had gone on ahead and my husband and I were lagging behind as I was heavily pregnant at the time and it was extremely hot weather. We were walking in an area of young trees so we could actually see into the woods for a fair distance from the path. It was at this point we heard the sound of cracking branches and looking up to his left my husband saw what he describes as a black animal, as large as a good sized dog, with very shiny black thick fur and a bushy tail, running head first down the trunk of a nearby tree (about 20–30 m away). He could clearly see it had wide paws, a thick-set neck area and a bushy tail. He likened its movements to that of a domestic cat running down a wall or tree; however, this was much larger and heavy-set. Unfortunately it was over very quickly and I did not look up in time to see it and it had by then disappeared into the overgrowth. However, I heard the sound it made as it came down the tree and it definitely sounded like something pretty large and several branches were broken on the tree.

Of course everyone made all the usual jokes and we put it from our minds as our baby was born shortly afterwards, etc. We were just watching a programme about Bigfoot this afternoon and we were reminded of this incident, and had a quick look on the internet to see if we could find anything similar and of course came across your site (the Dorset Big Cats Register). Sorry if it is so out of date that it is of no use to you, but we thought you may still be interested anyway.'

29 October 2006

A witness reported: 'I have seen today a large black cat possibly a panther on the road near Blandford in Dorset at 7.55 a.m. It was chasing a small deer across the road in front of me about 10 yards away. They both darted through a hole in the hedge and ran across the field. It was huge and had a very long tail. I could not see the head well as it was moving fast. I stopped the car and stood on the seal of my car door to see over the hedge and watched them move fast away. It was only about 5–10 seconds in total. I hope this helps some. I won't forget it, I know that.'

🐾 Bothenhampton

West Bay Road – 5 September 1995

The *Dorset Echo* reported: 'Retired merchant seaman Jack Bellarby of West Bay Road said he was quite amazed to see a large black animal pacing very slowly northwards from West Bay at about 8.20 this morning by the side of a long hedgerow. "It looked just like a black panther to me," said Mr Bellarby. "It was easily observable by eye, but just to make sure I looked at it through my binoculars." He called his wife who confirmed that it looked like a black panther to her too.'

June 2003

Mrs Betty Savory made the *Bridport and Lyme Regis News* on 6 June 2003 with an unusually close observation of a frighteningly large animal. It was a few days earlier that she had woken up in the night suddenly, and noticed the security lights were on outside. She told me: 'Thinking it was probably a fox I looked out of the window and was amazed to see a big, black animal clinging to the small ornamental crab apple tree outside, about 15 ft away.' The tree is only about 8 feet tall, and the branches start at about 5 ft 6 inches, and she described its head as being directly below where the branches start, between the trunk and a small swinging bird box attached to the branch, which would have been about 5 ft off the ground. Its haunches were on the ground the other side of the trunk which was about 7 inches in diameter, or conceivably that was its tail resting on the ground – she could just see black body without detail behind the tree. This would have made the cat's body about 4–5 ft in length, excluding the tail. Otherwise the cat was well lit by the security light. It had its paw raised as if about to claw at the bird box. She shone a torch in its face and saw 'a couple of yellowy eyes'. She shooed it and it bounded off in big, loping strides towards the field behind a row of garages. She said, feelingly, 'I hope it never comes back.' They have a cat … but it is old and was inside that night. The tree is used as a scratching post by local cats judging by the scars about 1 ft up the trunk. There was a fresh scratch about 4 ft up it, on

The tree outside Betty Stocker's house, showing fresh scratches

the far side, which could have been made by the cat-like animal she saw.

Mrs Savory's neighbour is a Mrs B. She is an elderly, vivacious lady and used to live at Conygar Park, the other side of Bridport, about 25 years ago, at which time a Mrs Snooks lived in the big house. A leopard, with spots, was seen for a few weeks, apparently coming for the bread they used to leave out for the badgers. Mrs Snooks had said to her, 'All sorts of animals do come up, but they don't do any harm'. Mrs B said 'the feeling was that someone had turned it out'.

21 June 2004

Alan McNamee of Bothenhampton reported an alarming experience: 'On Monday evening of this week, at 11.15 p.m., I was working in my office, at home, when I heard a very strange sound coming from the side of my house. It was a sound that I had not heard before. At first I thought it was foxes or badgers fighting, but this sound was of some animal in great pain. I went down the stairs, all the time I could hear this awful sound getting louder as I got nearer to the side door. I switched the outside lights on and opened the door to the outside; normally it would go quiet, and that would be the end to it. But it made no difference; something behind the hedge went on making this noise. First I found a stick just outside the door, so I threw it in the direction of the noise, it still made no impact. By this time I can remember saying to myself, "What the hell is going on?" I walked slowly up the five steps to the hedge, which was moving backwards and forwards very quickly. I could still not see anything, so then I leaned over. My god – less than 1 m in front of me was a big cat! In its mouth was a badger, still alive and screaming in pain, and the cat was big! Its tail was banging into the hedge less than 6 inches from my legs, its head was facing away from me, its hindquarters were clearly visible. It was pure black and just over a metre, with a tail as long again about 2 inches thick. I estimated its size against the size of the hedge, path and walls, and the fact I was so close. Its ears seemed to be pinned back and not visible. When it saw me it gave a growl which sounded deep and heavy, and chilled me to the bone. Within the time it takes to blink, it stood up, turned and leaped a good 4 ft over a bank. I can't remember how I got back into the house, but I was scared to put it mildly! I ran back upstairs and rang the police, and reported what I had just witnessed. The crazy thing about all of this is I'm a photographer, and for the last 2 years I have been trying to film a big cat – I never thought that it would come and visit me!

At 11.35 p.m. I decided to film the area where I had seen the cat, which took a great deal of will power! I leaned over the hedge and took one shot, then went back into the house, went upstairs, opened the skylight window and took two random shots of the woods, hoping I would get something. At first I thought I had got nothing, but on looking in greater detail some time later I noticed the red stains on the wall, from the first shot I took from leaning over the hedge. Then right in the centre of the picture, two pink objects can be seen – I believe this to be flesh from the badger.

On Tuesday morning at 8.15 a.m. the police arrived, we walked up into the garden, and I was telling the officer about the cat, when the officer looked down on some bonfire ash and noticed a cat print, about the size of a closed fist; it was hard to see a detailed impression because the wind had blown in some of the sides.'

The scene 20 minutes after the sighting of a big cat, showing possible fragments of badger flesh. (Photo credit: Alan McNamee)

🐾 Bournemouth

Manor Road - April 2005

Steve Moult was working as a security guard at a block of flats in Manor Road, Bournemouth. He reported: 'I saw a black panther on the CCTV at about 2.30 a.m. one night and didn't dare to go out for my hourly stroll around then!'

West Cliff Road -20 August 2005

The local press reported: 'Kevin Hamersley, 24, had been celebrating a friend's 21st birthday in Bournemouth, Dorset, when he spotted a puma prowling the West Cliff at around 4.30 a.m. on August 20. "It was as big as a dog, but it wasn't a dog," said the car spares salesman from Devizes in Wiltshire. He said he had been walking back to his hotel along West Cliff Road and looked down a street towards the sea. "It stopped in the middle of the road and looked at us for about 2–3 minutes. We were just trying to work out what it was and it just stood there frozen, looking at us, before it turned around and ran off. I thought it might be a puma. I watch a lot of wildlife programmes so I know my big cats. I don't think they would attack humans unless you provoked them, but they are meat eaters so I didn't hang around. I didn't want to get gashed by its big claws." He said he had only had a couple of drinks that night and was not drunk but was convinced the 2-ft-high cat, with a long thin tail that curled upwards, was either a puma or a lynx. According to Mr Hamersley the cat had dark brown fur on its back and face, with a lighter, sandy-coloured underbelly. "I'm now convinced there's either a puma or a lynx on the loose in Bournemouth," he added.'

Springbourne – November 2005

Renea Gascoigne reported: 'It was November 2005, towards dusk. Looking into a neighbour's garden we saw something move through it, about 30 ft away. It was too fast to get a very long look at it, but we had a good enough look to know it was a big cat. It was sandy in colour with no apparent markings, ears pointed, and the tail was thick and long. The animal was about the size of a large German shepherd dog but slightly stockier. We were too afraid to go into the garden to get any further evidence unfortunately!'

🐾 Bridport

Bridport and its surrounding villages have been something of a hotspot for big cat sightings for the past decade or more. Many of the encounters have been reported in the local newspapers, and some of the witnesses themselves have kindly supplied me with additional details. See also the multiple sightings to the south of Beaminster.

Allington Hill – Spring 1998

The witness, Stuart, did not see any animal on this occasion, but reported a slightly eerie experience. 'I was running on Allington Hill, Bridport, at about 3 p.m. in pouring rain and with very low cloud so that visibility was probably no more than 20 m. Whilst I was at the top of Allington Hill I became aware of movement, just outside the range of visibility, that seemed to keep pace with me as I ran. There was also a sound of breathing that I could not explain. I was satisfied this was not a person as the route taken would have silhouetted them against the skyline even if features would have been obscured. Something about the experience concerned me, and I left the hill towards the New Hospital as soon as possible. I later rationalised the encounter as being a symptom of overexercise.'

Allington Hill – 11 August 1998

The *Dorset Echo* reported: 'Welfare worker Jan Freeman had been walking her two terriers near the town's community hospital at 10.30 a.m. on Monday, when she noticed the animal staring at her just 50 yards away. She said the dogs saw the creature but did not react. Mrs Freeman said: "I couldn't believe it but it was as clear as day. I was just coming out of the shade when I saw about 50 yards from me a large, black cat-like creature – there was no mistaking what it was. It had a very long tail, its body was about 2.5 ft long and it was very low to the ground. It looked at me and slunk off

Allington Hill

into the undergrowth. … It was a wonderful thing to see; there is no doubt about what it was.'"

East Bridport – June 2002

Mr B was 'sitting in my lounge, enjoying the landscape, as I do every day', when in a field of sheep on the hillside opposite he spotted a 'pure black', cat-like animal stalking the sheep. He watched it for some time through binoculars as it crawled along, legs crouched, head lowered. It was the comparison with the sheep in the field that enabled him to gauge its length – 1.5 times that of a sheep. They took no notice though it was only about 50 yards from the nearest one, and it finally disappeared over the brow of the hill. 'The sheep didn't seem concerned. Perhaps they see it regularly?' he speculated. He reported it to the police. Some months later he and his wife thought they saw it again, on the brow of the same hill, but felt it was too far away and its identity therefore too uncertain to call the police again.

North Bridport – March 2003

A completely different animal was seen on the northern outskirts of the town by Mr and Mrs T. They had lived abroad and in Singapore for many years and had seen a number of big cats in the wild. In March 2003 they were alerted by the sight from their back window of a strange, cat-like animal ambling up the field which rises directly behind their house, about 40 yards away. Mr T ran upstairs to get a better look and saw it from behind as it disappeared over the edge of the rise. It was 'slightly smaller than an Alsatian but bigger than a retriever. My first thought', he said, 'was that it could be a dog – but it looked wrong. It had a stubby head; similar to a bulldog, but it was not a bulldog. It had a long tail. It was a sandy colour and its coat was mottled – not as with spots, but as if it could be moulting. The head and tail did not go with a dog.' There is an abattoir two fields away, in the direction it was going, and Mrs T wondered if 'it could have smelt the blood'. The horses in the next field seemed to be oblivious to it.

Mr T went out with binoculars and searched for 15 minutes, saw nothing more, and then called the police.

Askers Meadow – 11 July 2003

A month after Mrs Savory's sighting at Bothenhampton came the closest encounter yet with a large cat-like animal. It happened about half-a-mile as the crow flies from the previous sighting, in Askers Meadow, which comprises several water-meadows on the western outskirts of Bridport. The meadows are bordered by the river and the houses of the town on one side, and on the other by the ring-road. The old railway used to follow the route of the ring-road.

Karen Rees told me: 'I go for a walk on Askers Meadow every morning at 5.30 a.m. with my dog, Sunny, a large, black Labrador lurcher cross. I usually meet my Mum there who also has a black Labrador, Mia. Hers is very, very glossy because my Dad used to be a Metropolitan police dog-handler and buffs Mia up with chamois leather. We usually circle a long, thicket-style hedge between two meadows – she goes one way and I go the other and we meet the far side of the thicket. The morning of Friday 11th July 2003 was a beautiful morning and I was marvelling at it – everything was very still – and thinking vaguely about the day's work ahead. Then about 30 yards away, behind the barbed-wire fence at the edge of the thicket, I saw what I thought was Mum's dog, lying injured – a hind leg with a really glossy black coat. I went towards it thinking, "Oh God – that's Mia", but as I got closer I realised it was much too big to be Mia. It was lying completely motionless, but when I was within a few feet of it and just beginning to call "Mia", it sprang up. It went from lying down to all four paws in the blink of an eye! I didn't see it get to its feet – it was lying down one moment and the next it wasn't. I was near enough to have touched it. As it sprang up it bared its teeth at me and made a peculiar half hissing, half growling, guttural noise which I took to mean "Bugger off and leave me alone". I was more than happy to oblige!

The two things that most affected me were its eyes and teeth. I saw that the canines were about 2–3 inches long. Its eyes were a smoky amber colour – as if an orange had a grey veil over it, or, although it sounds clichéd, the same colour as the light vein of a piece of polished Tiger's Eye gem stone. It made a blood-curdling noise – neither a hiss nor a growl, but a very guttural noise, difficult to describe. It then turned and made off into the thicket, and I estimated its size as being three times the size of Sunny, not including the tail – and not including Sunny's tail. The tail was very long and hooked up at the end. Sunny had not seen the cat as he was chasing rabbits some

Karen Rees and her dog Sunny – the big cat she encountered was just behind the barbed wire fence

distance away, but when he got back to me he stayed very close beside me, which is most uncharacteristic of him, because he is the kind of dog who runs energetically about. When I got to the stile at the other side of the thicket I saw my Mum coming towards me with Mia, and looked about to see if I could see where the cat had gone. I just caught sight of its backside and tail disappearing into a hedge running at right angles to the original thicket, about 50 yards away. I told my mother what I had seen, but she had not spotted the animal as she walked round her side of the thicket.' Karen rang the police when she got home, but their subsequent search failed to find the animal.

Victoria Grove – April 2005

The witness was visiting a house at Court Orchard near North Allington. He saw from the kitchen window, which looks onto Victoria Grove, what he thought could be two calves at the top of a field of cows. 'The cows had legged it to the other end of the field, but I thought hang on a minute, when do calves stand up on their hind legs and have a sparring match?' Then he wondered if they could be black dogs playing. But it was their shape and manner of playing that convinced him otherwise. He breeds Dalmatians and is accustomed to watching dogs play. 'These were batting at each other, swiping sideways like a cat does, putting their heads to the side and swinging at each other.' He could see their long tails 'stuck up and waggling – they were big tails, swishing around everywhere, and when one was stalking the other its tail was dragging down touching the ground. I thought they're cats – pretty big cats at that distance.' He watched them for 4 or 5 minutes and finally one ran straight into the woods behind, and the other bounded after.

Disused railway line to West Bay – 16 June 2006

Brian Fisher recounted: 'Whilst visiting a relative in Bridport, my wife and I were walking between West Bay and Bridport on the disused railway track. We saw what we first thought was a fox about 40 yards ahead of us, walking away from us. It was sandy colour and definitely of the cat family but was too long in the leg for a domestic cat. My wife thinks that the tail was striped with white. It turned and looked back at us but did not seem bothered and soon disappeared to the side hedge. The location was where a newish housing estate bisects the track and where a pond is just off to the right.'

🐾 Broadstone

Silverdale Close – 18 October 2005

The *Dorset Echo* reported: 'Ten-year-old Nicholas Rogers from Poole got the shock of his life when returning home for his tea. As he ran from the recreation ground to Silverdale Close he saw a large black animal crossing the road towards him. He slowed to a walk and crossed over the road, coming to within 8 ft of the animal which stopped in the road and turned to look at Nicholas. He described the animal as a cat the size of a Labrador "with a large strange-shaped head and yellow eyes". It then turned and ran into bushes, Nicholas did the same and ran home. His mother said: "He's a sensible boy and not given to flights of fancy. I think he was a little scared when he got home. We have a cat at home, but he said the creature he saw was at least twice as big with a very smooth black coat."'

Springdale Road – 18 June 2006

John Pearman wrote: 'My wife and I were travelling by car at approximately 1.45 a.m. along Springdale Road into Broadstone when an animal sauntered across the road about 20 yards ahead of us. There is a bridle path known as the Roman road that leads up from some heathland above the Poole harbour area. The animal appeared to be taking the bridle path as its route. We both remarked how big a fox it was – then realised it was no fox. It was too long-legged to be a fox and appeared to be completely black with a long tail like a panther's (although slightly bushier). It was the size of an Alsatian dog and had slightly pointed ears (like a lynx?). Its face and muzzle weren't sharp enough to be a dog's or fox's. The animal was definitely black as it glistened in the light from our headlamps. Its body was definitely feline in shape. We stopped to watch it disappear into the shadows of the bridle path. Continuing down the road about a hundred yards further on we saw a fox on the pavement … totally different animal in size, colour and shape.'

🐾 Broadwindsor

September 1994

In September 1994 came reports of the creature the press dubbed the 'Beast of Broadwindsor'. Vincent Gavigan saw the cat-like animal one morning while delivering newspapers. He described it as 'as large as an Alsatian dog, with a puma-like head and green eyes'. It was within 40 yards of his car. It turned to look at him, jumped into the hedge and disappeared.

🐾 Bulbarrow Hill

Delcombe – 10 August 1995

On this day, two deer stalkers had such an extraordinary experience that one of them made detailed notes in his diary. This is his account: 'I had an evening stalk in Delcombe on the south-east side of Bulbarrow Hill booked for a friend and myself through the local agent. He confirmed that a number of roe bucks had been seen in the area the day before, and all but guaranteed that we would be able to take one or two. My friend, C.L., and I were experienced deer stalkers, and we set off stealthily from the road along a path which meandered through woodland until it came up to an enclosed grassy field. No beasts were seen on the walk, but no matter, this is where the roe would feast on the lush grass, and we could see the high seats located just on the edge of the woodland, placed where the deer were most likely to come out to graze, and where a safe downward shot could be taken. We worked our way just inside the woodland towards the seats, and took up our positions in plenty of time before dusk. We waited in long and agonising silence and expectation, until the light faded to such a degree that it was time to give up the expedition as fruitless, and for us to make our way back to the vehicles. The complete absence of beasts of any kind was somewhat surprising, and we ruminated on the situation as we marched boldly along the path, not worrying about the noise our boots made on the gravel, and half hoping to set a roe off, no longer shootable in the dusk, but just to prove that they were about.

As we were walking uphill on the last 200 yards to the road, I saw my car and, rather oddly, a bulky item on the boot thereof. Who had dumped a bag on my boot, and for what reason? When we had approached to about a hundred yards of it, the 'bag' slowly unwound and languidly lowered its front feet to the ground – whilst the rear of the animal, for such it was, remained on the boot. A sizeable beast! I immediately chambered a round in my rifle, and looked at the apparition through my telescopic sights. By then it had all four feet on the ground, its eyes glinting with a faint yellowish tinge, and looked for all the world like a black panther. It was hard to believe that such an animal was there right

Bulbarrow Hill, where Mike saw a panther climb off the boot of his car

in front of us, but my co-stalker and I agreed, with eyes firmly fixed on the cat, that that was the reason why we had seen no animals during our evening. I was ready to shoot the beast if it approached us, but when we were 50 yards from it, it turned and walked away slowly up the hill alongside my car, silhouetted on the horizon and no longer a safe shot, and into the woodland, out of sight. There was no doubt in our minds that we had seen a black big cat – a panther as far as I could judge.'

Delcombe Wood – 2002 and 2004

In 2002 the press reported that a very decomposed deer carcass had been observed lodged 15 ft up an oak tree in Delcombe Wood. On 10 November 2004 Dan Nathanson emailed the following additional information: 'I took an interest in the story because I own the wood and had noticed the carcass some weeks before, and had wondered how it got there. Incidentally, it was about 8 ft above the ground (not 15 ft) in the fork of an ancient beech tree (not oak). Deer jump high, but not into trees, and certainly not 8 ft high. I doubt whether it had been put there by a human as it would have needed a ladder and considerable energy to get it up there.' The press had speculated about whether the deer had been the prey of a big cat, since leopards habitually drag their kills up trees to remove them from other predators. Neither Mr Nathanson nor the press were aware at the time of the sighting of a panther-like big cat seen by the two deer stalkers in 1995.

🐾 Burton (Hampshire border)

19 August 2003

At 3 a.m. a woman was shocked to see a black, cat-like animal 'like a panther' cross the road only 50 yards in front of her car. 'It paused to look in my direction and then carried on walking. It wasn't too bothered by my presence.' The animal was approximately 2 ft high and 3–4 ft long. 'It had a long tail which hung down between the legs, shimmery, shiny, black fur and green eyes.'

1 June 2005

Aaron wrote: 'I was walking my dog and had just got back to the car this evening at about 8.30 p.m. when I saw a large dark-coloured cat in a field of immature wheat or barley. It was running in leaps and bounds towards a copse. The crop is about 3 ft high so it must have been a largish cat. It certainly wasn't moving like a dog and had a long tail. It was about 300 or 400 yards away from me but didn't seem to have seen me. Driving away from that spot I noticed near the copse a field with some horses in it. I usually walk my dog down that road, which is a quiet narrow country lane with minimal traffic, just east of the village of Burton. I was going to report it to the police, but decided not as they are pretty stretched as it is, and they probably wouldn't believe me anyway. I bought a great digital camera last Christmas and I usually carry it in my car – but the one night I forgot it I have a sighting!'

🐾 Burton Bradstock

Hawkins Barns – 9 September 1996

The *Dorset Echo* reported: 'The mysterious black beast of West Dorset has been spotted again. Giles Eastwood was walking his Alsatian Elias at dusk near Hawkins Barns on the lower road, about half a mile from Burton Bradstock, when he looked over his shoulder to see a huge puma-like creature slinking across a freshly cut cornfield. As he watched transfixed, the creature sank onto its haunches, sprang over a hedge and vanished. "I was confronted by something I could not comprehend initially", he said. "It had a very dark, silky body which certainly looked like a puma. It was very sleek and very elegant, and moved very gracefully. I only saw it for about 3 or 4 seconds. It was about three times the size of my dog. … I feel privileged to have seen it."'

Beach Road – 15 August 1998

The *Dorset Echo* again reported: 'Burton resident Ernest Foster was amazed to see a similar creature calmly crossing the road as he walked his retriever dog towards the beach area just after 7.30 p.m. The animal looked at him and then ran off into the gardens of properties in Beach Road. He said: "It was black and about 2.5 ft long with a very long tail. There was something about its eyes as well which made me think it wasn't just a cat."'

Bennetts Hill Lane – 1999

The witness, Stuart, wrote: 'I cannot remember the date, but it would have been late afternoon with the sun very low in the sky. I was cycling west along Bennetts Hill Lane when I noticed a disturbance in a group of cows further down the hill. For a moment I thought I saw a black animal moving fast about 20 ft from the cows, but I had sweat in my eyes which I wiped away. When I looked again the animal was not visible, but the cows were clearly still excited. I assumed this was either a dog or a trick of the light, but I have since seen cows confronted by dogs and they do not act the way I saw that day. On that occasion the cows seemed panicky and unsure of where to run.'

Burton Freshwater – March 2004

Trevor Ekins wrote: 'I enclose a couple of photographs taken at Burton Freshwater where the River Bride runs into the sea. The river was low and had left a soft mudbank. My eye was taken by a scatter of paw prints in the mud. The ground was impossible to walk in as my wellie prints show in the photo. I went home for my camera and returned. There were perhaps six or seven paw prints but mostly blurred, but I snapped the one clear one. My ruler shows it to be 6 inches at least across at its widest. The river was very low and a short, 6- to 8-ft mudbank was exposed sloping down to the water at about 10 degrees from the horizontal. To get there the animal would have had to leap down about 18 inches from the bank top. At that point there was a patch of gravel in the mud which gave a slightly firmer ground. There the mud ran out and presumably the animal leapt back up. The heavy disturbances at the top of the picture were my wellies, where I had gone down to have a look, but the mud was too soft and glutinous just there, so I leaped back up too! There were no prints from any other animal. I don't know what made those tracks, but the photos are genuine.'

Hive Beach – 25 May 2005

The witness lives near Hive Beach and reported: 'I was walking towards the village on the way to collect the children from school at about 10 past 3. I had just turned onto the main road heading east to Burton Bradstock, and looking through a field gate on the left I saw an animal about the size of an Alsatian bitch, which – initially by that big tail – I recognised as some kind of big cat. It was long and low to the ground with a really long tail and little pointed ears. It was a very dark brown with faint mottling. I had been thinking about something else, walking along in a daze until I saw it – thought "Oh wow!" – did a double take, and stepped back to take a longer look. I watched it sauntering along without a care in the world until it disappeared into

The gateway near Burton Bradstock where an ABC passed in May 2005

the hedge. I completely refuted my husband's subsequent suggestion that it might have been a large domestic cat!'

6 November 2006

Tara-Leigh Eggiman, a Coastal and Rivers Engineer, wrote: 'Our team would like to report a big cat sighting in Burton Bradstock, Dorset. At approximately 12.30 p.m., myself along with four other professionals (two from my company and two from the Environment Agency) saw what appeared to be a large black cat in an adjacent field. We were approximately 200 m away, but could see it moved very much like a cat (low to the ground), had a long tail and was quite slender. We watched the cat for about 5 minutes, and as we moved closer to the field boundary (the river) and continued to watch, it definitely became aware of us. It had the colouring, tail and build of a panther, but certainly not the size. I would say it was 1.5 m in length (head to tail) with body length of 1 m. The height I would put between 0.6 and 0.8 m. (Editor's note: this is well within the size of a 'panther' or leopard.) We have taken pictures, but again these are quite far away – but when you zoom in they are slightly better (see Introduction). The camera was a part of our professional field equipment (but only a basic digital camera, so not of great quality).We spent lunch in the pub where we heard local stories of others seeing this animal. After lunch we went back to the field where we saw the cat and found some paw prints (please see). The footprints were along the path it was travelling next to the shrub/tree line, so they were relatively easy to locate.

🐾 Canford Heath

Waterloo Road – 27 August 2002

The *Dorset Echo*, 27 August, carried this report: 'Post Office worker Bernard Seale, of Fortuneswell, Portland, was driving back home from work when he claims he saw the beast walk across the road in front of him, around 10–15 ft away from his car. Mr Seale said: "I have never seen anything like it before. I think it must have been either a puma or a lynx. I work nights sorting post at the Post Office mail centre in Poole and I was driving home around 3.15 a.m. on Waterloo Road, near Canford Heath, just outside, when I saw the creature walk across in front of the car. It was brown and had a tail with a white tip and it also had massive paws and walked like a large cat. I thought it might have been a fox as I often see them when I drive home from work, but as I put my full beams on I saw that there was no way it was a fox. When I saw its paws and its tail I knew that it was an animal I had never seen before."'

2005

PC John Snellin, Dorset Police's wildlife officer, said there had been a report of a big cat growling from inside bushes on Canford Heath in Poole at 8 p.m. A woman who works in the control room at Dorset Police reported hearing the noise as she was walking with her mother. Mr Snellin said: 'She was out walking with her mum and heard some growling behind the bushes. A loud roar like a big cat came from the bushes. They decided to run for it and as they ran off they heard another roar. She was a bit shook up.'

🐾 Canford Magna

8 June 2006

Alex Blainey was walking his dog at 7 p.m. with his partner. At the edge of a wood they saw a sandy-coloured big cat. 'It had a small head, long tail, and it was the way it ran – away then back. We were about 120 ft from it and it was in short grass. It was running around the edge of the wood, out of sight, then ran back into sight, then stopped. After 20 seconds or so it bolted off. It had a really small head compared to its body and very small, pointy-up ears. It was as fast as a greyhound … so majestic. It didn't run like a dog, but was very poised, graceful. The horses in the field took no notice.'

🐾 Cattistock

Autumn 1986

A witness wrote: 'In the autumn of 1986 I was walking with my baby in a pram on the road going from Maiden Newton to Cattistock, and had neared Cattistock going past a stretch of land that kept chickens on at the time. I saw what seemed to be a lynx. It was only a few feet away from me and walked quite slowly and stealthily across the field in front of me. Its appearance was tabby cat, the size of a large Labrador, with very upright pointed ears with long upright dark tufts. It looked right at me with a glare, very bright eyes. It held my gaze all the way across the field in front of me. The tail was bushy and long with dark stripes or rings, and dark at the tip (like a racoon's tail markings). I had a very good view of it it was so close to me and I didn't even think to be frightened!

I saw an article in the *Dorset Echo* May 21, 2005, in which a Dorchester resident had seen an animal described just like the one I saw, but he does not say what the tail was like. I had thought it was a Siberian lynx but the tail was too long.'

🐾 Charlton Down

Old Sherborne Road – 13 July 2006

Police officer Emma Hawkes recounted: 'I was riding my horse at noon along a bridle path near the Old Sherborne Road, Dorchester. My two dogs were 50 m ahead of me when a large golden-brown-coloured animal, approximately 6 ft long and 2 ft 6 inches to 3 ft high, crossed the path in front of us – about 6 ft in front of the lead dog. It had a long sleek body with a thick tail as long as the body, and a rounded head. My bitch initially thought it was a deer and chased after it into a field of oil seed rape, but lost it.

She returned a minute later and went off to her favourite pond for a swim as though nothing had happened. The horse wasn't spooked as we were too far away, and it didn't seem at all interested in the dogs or the horse. I looked for tracks, but the ground was far too hard, and the rape field it went into had no obvious damage. I did have a look at a photo of a puma on the internet later and it matched the shape exactly. It definitely was not a deer, fox, or dog. I am a police wildlife liaison officer for Dorset police and have heard of these sightings over the years. I am very glad to have seen one in the flesh.'

❧ Charlton Marshall

Disused railway line, near Hopegood Close – 31 October 2005

A witness reported: 'I have been told of a couple of sightings of big cats in the Blandford area. One of my colleagues was out with his wife on the disused railway line at the rear of Hopegood Close in Charlton Marshall near Blandford when they spotted a big black cat. He says it was too big to be a domestic cat and they had a good look for a couple of minutes before it moved off. Needless to say he now takes his digital camera with him in the hope of getting a picture. Unfortunately most of my other work colleagues have been taking the rise out of him, but it did prompt someone else to tell me of a sighting last year. He and his wife were looking out of a kitchen window in a house on Dorchester Hill near Bryanston, Blandford, and they both saw a large black cat crossing a nearby field. Both areas are fairly close to one another so it could be the same cat.'

Disused railway line – 7 July 2006

Kim Campbell was walking with his partner along the disused railway track at Charlton Marshall, near Blandford, at approximately 6.45 p.m. He wrote: 'Through a clearing looking onto a field, about 300 yards from us, I saw an animal lying down. At first we thought it was a fox. However, it was golden in colour, and when it sat up I could clearly see it was a large cat about the size of a large Labrador dog. It also had the same colouring as my Labrador dog but was feline, with pointed lynx ears. The animal began to clean itself as a cat would. My partner and I watched the cat for about 5 minutes – and it was not aware of us at first but after several minutes it spotted us, though did not seem too concerned by our presence. As we were only 2 minutes from home we went back to get our video cameras, but on our return the cat had gone. I contacted the Blandford police to inform them of my sighting.'

❧ Chideock

Golden Cap – Early August 2005

The *Dorset Echo* reported that a panther-like creature was seen by six members of the public at the Golden Cap caravan park, near Chideock. It was seen in a thicket about 200 yards from the beach. The creature was black, had a cat-like face and long tail.

🐾 Corfe Mullen

4 May 2006

A witness reported: 'I've just returned from the Purbeck area after a few days' break in a camper with my partner, and have just done a search on the web for "Dorset wild cat" … after a 'sighting' of something which really perplexed us on Thursday afternoon approx 13:00 on 4 May 2006. Whilst driving westbound along the A31 (at about 45 mph) near Corfe Mullen my partner said, "It's a big cat". I turned to look and caught a glimpse of what I can only describe as a black panther-type animal walking about 250 m away parallel with the road. My partner had a much better and longer sighting, as I was driving. I pulled into the nearest convenient point on the roadside – probably 200–300 m further down the road – and we both exited the camper to try and catch another sighting. After a few seconds we saw the creature walking towards some woods further away from the road. The second sighting lasted for about a minute but was restricted to only the top part of the creature as it was in long grass. If asked to describe the creature I would say: "Black cat, Labrador sized or larger, and looking remarkably like a panther". We both thought that by the way it moved, it was very definitely not a dog and very feline – something to do with the fluidity of movement in the rear haunch, and the ability to go at a lickety split pace, while remaining low to the ground. We are very sure it was a cat-type thing, based on the movement, and the speed yet fluidity with which it went through the grass.

We did consider reporting the matter to the police, but the whole episode seemed a bit surreal, and we had no "evidence". We have both heard stories in the news/press of various UK sightings of such animals and not taken them seriously … . We didn't fancy joining their ranks. I used to think it was all a load of old rubbish, Walter Mittys with nothing better to do, but now I look forward to getting myself a copy of your book and my next visit to Purbeck (with camera at the ready).'

🐾 Corscombe

Lower, Knapp and Underhill Farms – 25 February 2004

Paula Denham wrote: 'At around 9.00 a.m. last Friday I was walking my dog up a rough track in Corscombe and had not gone very far along the track when I heard the sound of loud purring seemingly coming from the hedgerow. It was far louder than the purr of a domestic cat and I felt half nervous and half intrigued. My dog had continued further up the track and I stayed around for a few minutes quietly trying to see into and along the hedge. After a couple of minutes the loud purring ceased and all was quiet. I continued the walk and when I got home told my husband.

Later that day I sat down to read the *Bridport News* and some headlines jumped out at me: "Wild beast of the West back again". I had not seen the beast, but it did sound very close and I wondered if the sound could have come from disused badger sets around there, in and close to the hedgerow; could it perhaps be using them for shelter? There were sheep and I believe baby lambs in fields belonging to Underhill Farm close by and I feared for their safety. I feel certain that all these stories are true because approximately 3 or 4 years ago my friend and I were walking in the vicinity and we both saw, at a distance of about 150 yards, the big, dark, slinking cat that others have reported. This was across fields between Lower Farm and Knapp Farm. It was so much bigger and longer than a domestic cat.'

🐾 Cranborne

Verwood and Alderholt – July 1999

A fair-coloured big cat was seen by a couple as they walked near Brockenhurst, Hants, in July 1999. The local press reported that 'since then the mystery creature has been spotted in Verwood and Alderholt.'

Edmondsham – October 2003

The *Dorset Echo*, 17 October 2003, reported: 'Police Officers Jon Kuspert and Richard Lill were out in Edmondsham patrolling for poachers when they spotted an unusual creature in their headlights. Jon said: "It took us both by surprise, it jumped out of a bush straight in front of us. We slowed down and followed it – at first I thought it was a badger but it moved like a cat. It had a long tail and a black stripe down its back – it was grey in colour and had coloured markings. I didn't know we had anything like that in Dorset – I used to work in Poole and never saw anything like that there. It was too big for a domestic cat. We came straight back and looked it up on the internet and the nearest thing to it is a European Wildcat. My colleagues are still taking the mickey out of me, but both of us saw it and we're certain of what we saw. I've been back to look for it since but couldn't find anything. We've had no reported problems of animals being attacked from farms."'

Boveridge – 27 June 2005

Mike Gardner wrote: 'My brother-in-law was travelling from Norfolk to visit my wife and me in Dorset on the night of 27/28 June 2005. He was driving across Martin Down (just in Hampshire) along the chalk track towards East Blagdon/Boveridge at 12.25 a.m. (28 June). When he was approximately 200 m inside Hampshire from the Dorset boundary at Bokerley Dyke he caught sight of a large black cat in his headlights crossing the track. It was the size of a medium-sized dog. It paused momentarily and looked towards his car. The eyes shone bright and yellowy before it moved off west to east. The approximate grid ref is SU054184. Hope this is useful.'

Edmondsham – Summer 2006

Mrs Cave wrote: 'My daughter saw a black cat in 2006 in the summer time on her way home at about 2 a.m. It crossed the road going towards Edmondsham. It turned its head and looked at her in the car and then carried on. It was bigger than a Great Dane with a short tail, about half the size of a domestic cat's tail. She got to about 5 m away from it. And the place where she saw it was the main Wimborne to Cranborne road, where there used to be a sign, but all that's left of that sign now is just two posts … as a new one has been put in just after it.'

Rye Hill – 22 October 2007

The witness wrote: 'It was about 10 p.m. and I and three others were driving home on the main road from Wimborne to Cranborne from an evening out. Just before the turning to go to Verwood we saw what we first thought was a fox crossing the road. On looking again we all said "that's not a fox, it's too big and the wrong colour". It did not stop, just carried on crossing the road – did not even look at the car. It seemed to be in a hurry.

My older daughter said she saw the black cat a couple of years ago when she was returning home from a night out, but never reported it as we all teased her about it. Her sighting was along the same road but further up, near the crossroads where one road goes towards Edmondsham (left) and the other that goes towards Sixpenny Handley (right) going towards Cranborne.'

🐾 Crossways

Railway line and Dick o' th' Banks Road – July 2001

The *Dorset Echo*, 15 August 2001, reported: 'A cat described as "completely black, and bigger than a German shepherd dog" was seen heading towards the railway. A woman walking her dog claimed to have spotted a large black cat run off into fields near the railway line at Crossways. The sighting came before eleven chickens and three ducks were killed by a predator in an overnight raid on a back garden in Dick o' th' Banks Road. Now police are urging anyone with sightings of animals that may pose a risk to the public to report them. The woman whose chickens were killed said her birds were targeted on five different nights. She said: "The animal would have needed to have been pretty big to get over the fence and take the ducks. Two chickens were left and they were torn across the chests and backs. I think it was the black panther a woman saw near the railway line as a fox couldn't have managed it." Another woman's dog was left cowering after they disturbed a large black cat near railway lines. A similar animal was reported 5 months later, near a quarry. It was "black, the size of a retriever, with short legs".'

Moigne Combe – January 2004

Richard Peacocke reported: 'Early this year, in January, I was walking my dog across fields near Crossways, just east of Dorchester. At one point there was a field laid to grass about 300 m wide leading to an ancient gateway without a gate into a further arable field. It was across this standard-width (3 m wide) gap that a large black cat passed into view. It was moving carefully – slinking – right to left towards rabbit warrens in the old ruined stables. It was the typical shape of a big cat, with low head and long tail. It was about a metre long, excluding the tail, and half that to the shoulder. I could judge that by the size of the gateway which it filled to a third as it slunk past. It was black – dead black – with small ears and a big muzzle. It had heavy legs, a solidly built body and a long heavy tail drooping in a crescent to its tip. We moved forward to see if a trail had been left, but there were no hairs or paw prints in the area. Why didn't I have my camera!'

Richard Peacocke's terrier Jack in the gateway where the big cat passed. (Photo credit: Richard Peacocke)

Hybris Business Park – 11 November 2004

Richard Peacocke again spotted the big cat crossing a road at 9.27 p.m. He wrote: 'It was a large black cat, and in comparison with road lines/kerb distance, must have been some 3 m long including the tail. Tail signature low, like a puma, with a "hunkered" neck and shoulders in proportion to length. It was crossing the entry of Hybris Business Park, Crossways, near Dorchester. The cat moved silently, stealthy and confident, from left to right (towards Moigne Combe, the site of the previous sighting) and slipped into the woods. My dog followed the scent trail into woods but returned when he came to the fence on the other side at the edge of a field.'

Dick o' th' Banks Road and Egden Glen – February 2006

Claire Spackman reported: 'My parents live in Crossways and are friends of the lady that spoke of her chickens and ducks being taken in 2001. I was speaking to my parents just the other day and a friend of my Mum's had told her that last month (February 2006) she had been walking her dogs in the fields out the back of Dick o' th' Banks Road (the council are now building houses on that land) and a big black cat walked across her path heading into the Egden Glen wooded area. Luckily the dogs were walking behind her sniffing at the ground; otherwise they might have chased it! As I didn't speak to the lady in person I do not have an exact description of what she saw, but there is always talk in the village of the black cat. Before building began in this field there were a lot of deer to be seen, which I presume would have been good feed for a large mammal, but they now have moved on because of the building. My parents' house is on Dick o' th' Banks Road, and for years I've looked out into the fields and seen nothing but average wildlife and the odd dog or cat. But it does seem that there are too many sightings for something not to be there. I hope this story is of interest to you.'

Moigne Combe – 14 August 2006
A witness wrote: 'I live in Moreton and my husband is working in Moigne Combe. The house where he is working has had deer trouble in the new landscaped gardens and a man was employed to spend the evening there to try and shoot the deer. While waiting for the deer to turn up he saw a large black panther-like animal and I think was rather freaked out.'

Station Road, Moreton – 20 January 2008
Two witnesses were in Station Road at 2 p.m. when they saw a cat 'about the size of a Labrador, but lower to the ground, and moving in a distinctive feline way. It was black with no markings, with a tail about 2 ft long. My daughter and I were riding on the road. The cat was about 40 m away on the other side of a thin hedge, moving deliberately across open flat ground. We wondered at first if it was a dog, but it was moving differently and the tail twitched. Its face was also too flat for a dog. We observed it for perhaps 20 seconds, and then spent some time debating what we'd seen. When we returned, it had gone.'

🐾 Donhead St Mary (Wiltshire border)

Ferne, Berwick St John – no date available
A police report read that a large black cat was seen crossing the road.

29 June 2003
A witness reported: 'I was driving through Donhead St Mary on the Dorset/Wilts border when this very large cat crossed the road, purposefully but unhurried, in the full beams of my car. I had about 5 seconds to watch it cross the road as I approached it very slowly, before it disappeared in the alleyway between houses in the village, leading off to fields. I had to stop to gather my disbelieving thoughts. The animal was approximately 40 inches long and 18–24 inches high. I am not sure of the tail length, but it was low-lying rather than straight out. The body colour was grey with mottled darker patches.'

Semley (Wiltshire border) – November 2007
A black big cat was seen in broad daylight and reported to the police.

 Dorchester

Weymouth Avenue – 28 November 2002

Andy Garrett called police on his mobile phone at 8 a.m. after spotting a large black cat, approximately 200 yards away, running at high speed across fields by the A37, a quarter of a mile south of Dorchester Football Club's ground on Weymouth Avenue. The field was grass about 8 inches high, and the cat was about the size of an Alsatian dog. He said: 'It was chasing something – zigzagging about in the middle of the field. It was pure black, cat-like in movement, and its most noticeable feature was its tail which was as long as its body and swept down to the ground and up again in a U-bend'. Andy is interested in wildlife, keeps dogs and cats and was adamant that the animal he saw was none of these, stating 'The fact that it was a big cat was as plain as the nose on my face'. The viewing lasted only about 15 seconds, but he said: 'It is still etched on my memory because it was a startling sight.' A squad car was dispatched after the call, but officers were unable to trace the mystery beast.

Morngate Caravan Park, Bridport Road – February 2004

Debbie Sparks is in the habit of popping outside for a cigarette. One night in February her attention was drawn to a caravan about 30 ft away, whence came the sound of cats. She saw two glowing eyes of a yellowy-green colour. The night was dark, so they were not reflecting some other light source: 'It was as if they were fluorescent. I couldn't take my eyes off them, they were horrible.' She went in to get a torch, and in the light of the beam she saw the animal was under the neighbouring caravan, where there is a space about 2 ft high. It was about the size of a small Alsatian, but stockier, with a longish tail. She said, 'I've never seen anything like it.' It had apparently got hold of a local black and white moggy but had let go because that ran off. She expected the animal to flee from the light too, but instead it started to walk towards her. She went inside hurriedly. The moggy appeared completely unharmed, and the mystery feline has not been seen since.

Poundbury Camp and railway line – 11 August 2004

Spencer Allen lives in Oxfordshire and works in Dorset. He reported: 'It was 11.50 a.m. and I was driving on the B3147 heading towards Dorchester and only about half a mile from the town. There are open fields on the right, divided from a steep hill by a railway track running parallel to the road. I saw a black cat-like animal running diagonally down the hill towards the railway line. It ran like a cat and had a very long tail. I slowed down and watched it for about 10 seconds. At that moment a train came along, going the other way. Its size enabled me to gauge the size of the cat, and I thought "God, that was big!" I estimated its size to be just over a metre. Its tail was smooth-looking and about 70 cm long, and curved down and up again in an S shape. The train obscured my view of the cat, and when it had passed the cat had gone. I was surprised to see such an animal so near to the town.'

Sherborne Road – April and 5 May 2005

In late April, Mr and Mrs Aylott were walking along a bridle path just off the Sherborne road at 9.30 a.m. when they spotted a black big cat lying by the side of the woods. At first they thought it looked like a calf, but it slunk off, moving in a cat-like way and showing a very long tail. It was about the size of a retriever. Then on 5 May they saw it again. They were walking their dogs on the same bridle path where they had seen it first; this time the cat was in a field closer to the road. It ambled across the path and into a gap in the hedge.

Road between Dorchester and Milborne St Andrew – May 2005

The *Western Gazette*, 22 February 2007, reported that in May 2005, a Blandford woman saw a large feline cross the road as she drove towards Dorchester from Milborne St Andrew late at night. Teaching assistant Ruth Steele said its belly was above the long grass on the verge, and it had a long tail with a distinctive rounded end.

Alington Avenue, Max Gate – 21 May 2005

The *Dorset Echo* reported: 'Max Gate, where Hardy wrote *Tess of the d'Urbervilles, Jude the Obscure* and *The Mayor of Casterbridge*, has become the latest location to be noted in the *Dorset Echo's* big cat diary. A Dorchester resident told police he saw a tabby cat "the size of a large Labrador with pointed ears" in Alington Avenue late at night. The animal glared at him before scaling the wall of Hardy's famous home and disappearing into the night. Andrew and Marilyn Leah have been the tenants of the National Trust property since 1994, when the couple were responsible for opening it to the public for the first time. The big cat sighting bewildered Mr Leah, who said: "It's news to me, I can't say I've seen anything myself. We do have a cat called Henry who is the star of the National Trust tea towel, but he's 16 and ambles around the grounds agedly. I can't imagine him leaping over walls at all." PC Paul Holman said the man who reported the sighting was scared by what he saw. He said: "We took the report seriously and searched the area but nothing was found."'

Talbothays Road, near St Osmund's School – 14 July 2006

The *Dorset Advertiser* reported: 'Marjorie Nicholson had woken at 4 a.m. and got up to see what the weather was like. "I opened the curtains and there coming in from the south end of Talbothays Road was what looked like a panther. It walked across the children's play area and then crossed the road, disappearing from sight in the direction of St Osmund's Middle School. It was about a metre long, a beautiful animal and had a beautiful stride – like a strut. I would say it was a panther. I did wonder if I was dreaming, but I wasn't. I watched it for a few minutes before it disappeared." She added: "The worst thing was my camera was in the cupboard next to me, but I couldn't take my eyes off it to get a picture."'

Dorchester Football Stadium – 30 August 2007

The *Dorset Echo* reported: 'A mystery big cat animal has been spotted in a field on the outskirts of Dorchester. Mark Dawson … said: "I was in the passenger seat as we approached the roundabout near the stadium and I was looking out for buzzards on fence posts. There was a short gap in the fence and I saw this animal standing on a slight mound in a field. It was about the length of half a football pitch away from me and I had a clear view of it. It was all black and had all four feet close together, the way a cat sometimes stands. It was definitely a cat of some kind, but it was the size of a big dog. It had a long tail with a curl at the end." He added: "I am absolutely 100% sure that what I saw was a panther. It wasn't a case of it could have been or looked a bit like one. The car was in a queue of slow-moving traffic and I had about 3 or 4 seconds to look at it. Unfortunately we couldn't stop or I would have grabbed the wife's mobile phone and taken a picture. But it's possible that other people were looking across through that gap on Sunday morning and saw it as well.""

Dorchester Football Stadium – 12 October 2007

A witness reported: 'I have just arrived at work having taken the No. 31 bus service from/to Weymouth. Whilst I was on the bus, just after passing the roundabout near the football stadium, in the first field to the right (about 8.05 a.m.) I spotted a big cat! It was stood in the middle of the field, facing towards Dorchester about 200 m away from the road. It was pure black, with a really long tail and I would say just bigger than an Alsatian dog. I had about 4–5 seconds to look at it and it was beautiful! Hope you can add this sighting to your history. I am aware that there was another sighting in the same area about a month ago, reported in the *Dorset Echo*.'

🐾 Durweston

Shaftesbury Road and Durweston Bridge – 29 February 2005 and summer 2004

A witness wrote: 'I'd like to report a sighting of a panther on our farm yard last night. We live on the higher Shaftesbury road about 3 miles from Blandford. My husband went to put out the rubbish last night at around 8.30 and standing at the rear of our car was a large cat who stood there staring at him. It then turned and ambled slowly off towards the adjacent cattle barn (empty) and off to the fields. I also saw one basking in the sun above the Durweston Bridge lights last summer – presumably the same animal. There is also a very strong cat urine smell in various locations in and around the barns on this land and I did think that was strange as we only have dogs.'

Durweston Mill – 2 September 2006

The *Western Gazette*, 22 February 2007, reported: 'The sighting and capture on camera of a large black cat-like animal near Durweston has renewed speculation that a "big cat" is roaming the area. The beast was spotted in September 2006 by Mrs "Dumps" Ryall of Durweston Mill, who said: "I was looking out of the window across the meadow when I saw it. I grabbed a camera and took these quick shots. I didn't have time to change lenses, but the photographs clearly show a large cat as big as a good-sized Labrador. I haven't seen it since." Her pictures show the animal close to an electric fence battery case which measures more than 18 inches in height, with a rabbit in the foreground, suggesting that it stands nearly 16 inches to its shoulders, much bigger than the average cat. And it has added weight to the claims of four Blandford School pupils, one of them her son, who said a couple of years ago they chased a large black cat over rough ground in the village, and watched it try but fail to bolt down a badger sett.

Jon Ryall, then 14, said he was out with three friends, Dwayne Lewis, Ross Beaumont and Lloyd Boyle, when they saw the animal a few hundred metres from the mill. "We were walking in what is known as the valley when we all saw this large

Photo credit: Mrs 'Dumps' Ryall

black animal about 20 m away. We all agreed it must be the panther which had been in the news, so we followed it, and got within 4–5 m when it started to slink off. It was huge. It turned and saw us and snarled, then bolted towards the badger sett, but was too big to get down the hole. It ran up the side of the bank and disappeared into the shrubbery."

Lloyd said: "We are all in the Blandford Air Cadets, so we have a bit of outdoor training, and are taught to observe things. But we were all amazed at the size of the beast. It was nearly as tall as a sheep, but a little longer and slimmer. It was beautiful, and obviously a member of the cat family."

Mrs Ryall said: "I'm sure the one I saw must be from the same family, if not the same cat. A number of people in the village have seen it, but keep quiet because they don't want people to think they are bonkers. I watched it walk halfway across the field before it struck me that it was rather large and I grabbed my camera."

The latest big cat sighting follows a number of similar sightings in recent years. They include sightings by a group of men out rabbiting from Bagber and Fifehead Neville who chased it after it ran towards the headlights of their Land Rover. Another sighting was reported by a retired company director from Winterborne Stickland. '

🐾 East Stour

Village churchyard – Summer 1994
A man saw a large black cat in daylight in the churchyard at East Stour. It was also seen crossing a field by two men who were interviewed in Motcombe by Meridian News.

Marnhull Road – Spring 2001
Jim Talbot recounted: 'On a Saturday afternoon sometime in the spring-time of 2001 we were travelling from Marnhull in a Landrover Defender and so had good visibility over hedges into nearby fields. Just past the Todber bend towards East Stour, no more than half a mile further on, I saw a big cat moving in typical cat mode around the edge

of a field to the east of the road. I fairly quickly registered that it was much larger than a domestic cat – sleeker, scoop-backed with a large scooped tail held out horizontally behind. I was the only one to spot it unfortunately, but our vehicle was no more than 20 m from the beast and it was therefore very easy to get an idea of the size (about two or three times as big as a large domestic cat). It was sleek, jet black and really shiny black as if the coat had a conditioner! I'm a biologist by training and I recognised it to be a panther-type of big cat. No doubt in my mind. I reported it to the police and then to a friend, a local farmer with livestock, who then told us there had been a number of sightings. Shortly after, the local paper carried a letter from a local retired farmer who had also seen a similar beast nearer to Gillingham.'

The churchyard in East Stour

🐾 Eype

Higher Eype – 1983

A light brown, puma-like big cat was seen in daylight by a knowledgeable witness. Sally Gale passed on this interesting early sighting: 'A friend of my father's saw a large sandy coloured animal running towards my father's field at Higher Eype, near Bridport. The friend said that he saw it leap across the hedge and into my father's field. My dad went to investigate and saw massive footprints, and where the animal had jumped across the hedge it was totally flattened. Ironically enough another friend of my dad's had recently been abroad studying pumas and said that the footprints definitely looked very similar to that of a puma/mountain lion. Needless to say my dad returned to his field many times, but with a gun! Just in case.'

Sluice Hill – 2002

Sally Gale has had three glimpses of large feline animals in the area over several years. The latest was on Sluice Hill. 'That was a very large, feline animal that was creeping low to the ground as if stalking something. All three of these sightings have left me with hair quite literally standing up on the back of my neck.'

❧ Ferndown

River Stour, Longham – 1990s
Jonathan McGowan, one of Dorset's leading wildlife experts, surprised a puma drinking from the river. He and three companions had walked over a footbridge to a small island in the River Stour when they spotted the animal. He warned his friends to stand aside so as not to block the animal's escape route. Sure enough the puma made a dash for it back along the footbridge, but half way across it seemed simply to vanish before their amazed eyes. Mr McGowan ran to the spot in disbelief and found one wet, puma-like footprint on the wooden boards. Three years previously, in the 1980s, he had seen a puma stalking a badger near Blandford.

February 2003
A black, panther-like cat was seen twice in Ferndown. The two sightings were only half a mile from each other.

St Leonards – 17 July 2004
Mr C sent the following report: 'It was the early hours of July 17. I work at night and drive home the same way every time. It was first light – I had night sky behind me and morning sky in front of me. I was approaching St Leonards on the A31 dual carriageway, going towards Ferndown. I had just cornered the small roundabout when I braked hard – because there sitting in the middle of the carriageway was what I believe to be a leopard type of big cat. It scared the life out of me. It was about 40 ft from me for about 10–20 seconds. Then, in one movement, it leaped/bounded into side bushes about 14 ft away. I think it was watching the kennels nearby. I have looked through your website and it most resembles a leopard. It was solid at the shoulders, sitting about a metre tall; its tail was 3–4 ft long. I have been doing that journey for 7 years mainly at night-time and I have seen all sorts of strange things, but not like this. I am sure it was no dog or household cat. I said to myself that if I saw a police car on the rest of my way home I would stop to report it, but I didn't.'

Longham Lakes – May 2007
Simon wrote on behalf of Matt: 'I'm writing on behalf of my friend. About 2 weeks ago down by Longham Lakes, the new reservoir near Ferndown, he was walking back, cutting across the field, when he froze as he saw a large, black, very silent creature which he recalls to be bigger than his Alsatian dog. It was about 20 ft away on the other side of the gate. The creature ignored him, and went running on past. It looks as if it could be the Longham panther we had both heard so much about. It was not a dog or fox – it was the panther!'

🐾 Frampton and Southover

1995

A motorist driving home to Cerne Abbas saw a long dark tail, which looped down and up again, disappearing into a roadside hedge near Frampton. It was dark at the time.

Southover – July/August 2004

The witness owns a flock of geese, and for this reason, he says, he is familiar with every possible predator for miles around and has shot most of them. It was while he was tending to the geese one morning at 7 a.m. that he saw a black cat, 'Alsatian-sized but longer' which looked at him and then returned the way it had came – around a large, disused slatted cowshed. He also connected this cat with one of his geese killed in an unusual way – bitten through the breast bone. There were no black domestic cats in the village.

Metlands Wood, Southover – Summer 2005

Daphne Hawkins spotted a big cat crossing a field adjacent to Metlands Wood.

🐾 Hartland Moor

Hartland Stud – 2001

A witness reported: 'I do think I saw (a black panther-type cat) on two occasions on Hartland Heath. It was near Hartland Stud just down from the Halfway Inn.'

2000 and 15 April 2004

The *Bournemouth Echo* reported: 'Three friends out walking together on Hartland Moor, Purbeck, believe they witnessed two big cats resembling pumas tumbling out of a tree. The incident happened in broad daylight and one of the party snapped a photo of a 3-inch paw print on her mobile phone. Chris Austin and his wife Sandy from Merley could hardly believe their eyes. He said: "You hear about big cats and read about them, but you don't expect to see one yourself and certainly not two of them together. We really didn't expect to see things like that in the countryside. It was broad daylight and before falling out of the tree there was a screeching noise, it was an eerie noise, not something you get from a domestic pet." Fellow walker Mrs Hayes, from Poole, said: "We heard a very loud cat screech which made us look up. It must have moved because it saw us coming and moved too quickly as the branch broke and two cats tumbled out of the tree in a panic. The tree was about 40 yards away and I was rooted to the spot – I just didn't believe it. I turned to my friends and asked 'Did you see that?' and they had. One cat was very black and the other was slightly browny-black – they were both about the size of a young Labrador with very long tails. We weren't frightened as it was just so amazing you don't get time to think about it."'

Sandy Austin had had a previous sighting: 'Four years ago I saw another one. I was taking the dog for a walk at night in April. We live in a cul-de-sac and from that there is a path leading to a green which was well lit. I heard something and wondered if it was a deer, but there was no sound of hooves. Nor was it a fox. Then I saw a black cat come out of the woods about 70 yards from me.

Talking to my friend and saying I saw some cats he said to me he'd seen a black cat a few years ago too. He is a crab and lobster fisherman and was fishing around Lulworth under the cliffs pulling in pots and saw it on a ledge in the cliff. He and his three fellow crew members watched it for 20 minutes lying in the sunshine.'

🐾 Hinton, Christchurch (Hampshire border)

24 November 2006
Richard Kittle wrote: 'It was 8 p.m.-ish on a dark, windy, rainy coldish night and I had just driven home. I was just turning into my drive when I saw an animal, dark coloured but not black, by the side of the road – I thought eating something. I couldn't think what it could be. A goat? A deer? – though it did not move like a deer. I parked and went into the house and said to my wife, "There's something in the bushes" and went out again on foot for a closer look. I got to about 5 yards from it. It looked like a cat the size of a good-sized Labrador – 3 ft long, with big, pointed ears and a long tail curled up in a loop. We looked at each other for about a minute before it bounded off into the bushes. In the last few days our dogs have been unusually barking, and I had thought there may be deer or a fox about.'

🐾 Hurn, Bournemouth Airport

Industrial estate near the airport – 14 August 2005
The local press reported: 'An employee at a scaffolding company reported defending himself with a large piece of wood after sighting a black panther at an industrial estate near Bournemouth International Airport on 14 August. "If he went so far as to pick up a bit of wood, he obviously saw the thing and was quite concerned for his own safety," added Dorset Police Wildlife Officer John Snellin.

Mr Snellin said there were around thirty reported sightings of big cats in Dorset every year, with "fairly regular reports of European lynx cats in Weymouth."'

Spur Road – 26 August 2006
Jonathan McGowan filed this report with the Big Cats in Britain research group: 'My brother telephoned me excitedly early one morning. It is the first sighting of a wildcat he has ever had. David McGowan, a taxi driver, was taking two ladies to Ringwood from Bournemouth, when just outside Bournemouth, a large, greyish animal started to cross the dual carriageway, but changed its mind; in mid lane, it turned around and ran back into the bushes. It had trotted slowly towards the central reservation

before doubling back; it was approximately 30 yards in front of the car. Dave saw it first and described it as "a large dog-sized animal with large ears, long thickish legs, with a bouncing sort of trot". He didn't notice a tail, and at first never even recognised it as being a cat because of this. Only when it hesitated at the road side after doubling back did he and the two passengers notice that it wasn't a fox. One lady said it "looks like a lion". The other woman said it was probably a big fox, but apparently she never took much notice of it. Dave said, "It's a cat", and at that point telephoned me.

In the morning I went to the exact spot … and later on investigated the area myself. What a surprise, the lynx was still there! Curled up under brambles just 4 m from the dual carriageway. It slunk away into the undergrowth at my approach. There was no chance of a photo, as it was always obscured and I was only seeing little bits of the body at a time. The area is on a golf course, alongside a river, lots of rats, rabbits and foxes to eat. The animal I saw was rather small, more likely a female, and the size of a Springer spaniel.'

Matchams Lane – 1 November 2007

Someone reported: 'I am an Air Traffic Controller at Bournemouth Airport and I received a call from the police control room at Winfrith to say that they had just had a call from a woman, reporting a big black cat in the Matchams Lane area at the end of runway 26. She informed the police that it was on the airport perimeter and definitely not a domestic cat or fox as it was too big. She was adamant it was a big cat. This happened at approximately 12.30 a.m. when she was driving home. I subsequently contacted security at the airport and was informed by the security guard that there have been numerous sightings recently, especially to the north of the airfield in the heathland within the airport grounds where not many people go. He himself told me that he'd seen something whilst out on his security patrol recently.'

🐾 Kingston (Hampshire border)

South of Ringwood – May 2001

It was a bright morning in May or June and Mrs Welsh was driving with her 12-year-old daughter on a single-track road near Kingston. She said: 'We came around a slight bend to see a big, jet-black cat emerge from the left-hand side hedge and stop in the middle of the lane. It didn't move so I had to stop the car. The cat was standing there only about 2 ft from the bonnet. It is a Nissan Serena – a biggish car – and it was at least the whole width of the car. It had huge paws, a long tail looped up at the end, a panther-like domed head, and amber eyes. It stayed completely still in front of the car looking at us for about 30 seconds I should think, though it seemed like an eternity, and then sauntered off to the right, with distinctively feline body movement. It was completely bizarre. My daughter and I looked at each other in stunned silence as it came out of the hedge; it was quite frightening, and I know it was silly but I locked the car door. You just don't see something like that. I had never been interested in them till then. I rang the police, and also told the people at the riding stables who said they knew of similar sightings.'

Stony Lane – 29 July 2005

Symon Clarke reported: 'My brother is a local taxi driver in Bournemouth. In the early hours of 29 July he was travelling in his taxi along the B3347 Stony Lane towards Ringwood when he saw a large black cat emerge in front of him, run across the road, and disappear into the hedgerow on the other side. He described it as a large black cat similar to a panther and stated that it had very large, muscular shoulders and paws.'

🐾 Lower Bockhampton

West Stafford – 1994

Tamara Loakes encountered a big cat at very close hand in 1994, just outside West Stafford, a small hamlet 2 miles east of Dorchester. She said: 'I was cycling back from Dorchester one calm and mild summer night at around midnight, when, as I descended the slope having just gone over the railway bridge, I had to brake quite hard to stop myself colliding with a medium to big animal. The animal, which looked uniformly black in the light cast by my bike lamp, moved slowly and unhurriedly across my path, from a wire fence bordering a large field to my right and disappearing in undergrowth bordering another field on the other side of the road.

Initially and naturally, for the first few seconds, I assumed it was either a badger, deer or large fox, even a dog. However, it did not move like or had the shape, or GIS, of any of these and it was certainly vastly bigger than a domestic cat. Being a zoology graduate, and having spent a career studying and interpreting wildlife, I was perhaps in a better position than many to judge the type of animal passing almost ghost-like a few feet from the front wheel of my bike. So although it was a dark night in an unlit area of the countryside, I realised, with mounting incredulity, that it was a big cat. By the time I had registered what it was, the back half of the animal glided away to my left silently. I watched the long slim curved tail follow the rest of it, then it was gone.'

Lower Bockhampton – 26 May 2006 – and Yeovil – October 2003

Paul Gray reported: Every night and most mornings I take a jog from Dorchester going out towards West Stafford. Before Stafford House I turn towards Lower Bockhampton. It was about 8.30 on the evening of this encounter. Just before the bridge at Lower Bockhampton there is a path that runs parallel to a stream. When I was around half way down the path I noticed there were some abnormally sized pad marks in the mud and that there was still water around the upturned edges of the smeared pad marks. For some reason I looked to the right of me and saw a collie-sized lynx staring at me on the other side of the stream. It was a sandy colour, with white rings around the eyes, and was about 18 inches tall and about 2.5 ft long. It had pointed ears with black tufts on the ends of about 3 inches long and had a small, black-looking tail. The cat and I stared at each other for about 10 seconds when it crouched down as if to pounce. At this point I shouted at it and it stared at me angrily, then bounded away without making any sound.'

Curiously enough, Paul had had an encounter with a puma-type big cat 3 years previously. Although it took place in Somerset I include it as it was one of the closest sightings of a puma on record. This is the report he filed at that time: 'I go to boarding school in Somerset. One night in late October 2003 at around 9 p.m. I was driving my car on a country road when I saw a pair of yellow eyes in the distance. I was travelling at about 50 mph and had my full-beam headlights on; therefore I thought that the animal would move out of the way. However, instead it ran towards the car. As you can imagine I panicked and performed an emergency stop. The area that I did the emergency stop in was a farm entrance, heavy in mud. The car slid around in the road through 360 degrees and then stopped. I then looked to see what had happened to the animal and was scared to find it looking at me through my car window (it is a sports car that is low to the ground). The cat was then distracted by something on the farm and ran off into the farm dairy area. The following day I contacted the police at Yeovil which is only about 7 miles away. They told me I was the sixth person to report seeing a large cat in that area, but didn't seem interested. The cat that I saw was a puma. It was about 5 ft long with light-brown short fur and a very muscular body. The facial markings were very distinctive.'

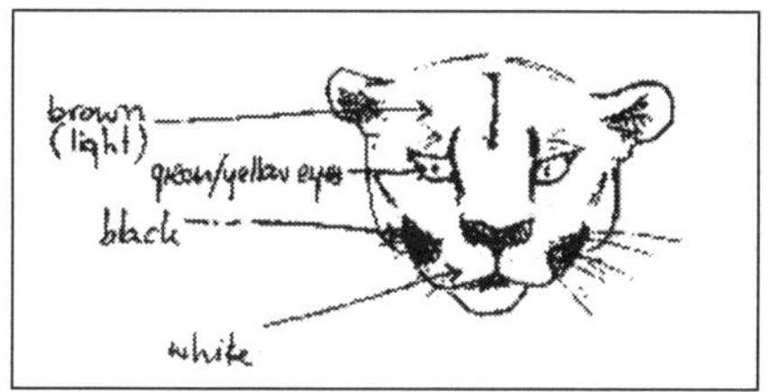

Detail of Paul Gray's drawing following his encounter with a puma. (Credit: Paul Gray)

🐾 Lulworth

White Nothe Cliffs – 1960s

Retired fisherman Jim Miller, who lives in Lulworth, recalls seeing 'a bloody great cat' picking its way along White Nothe cliffs near Lulworth in the 1960s. 'It was near enough the size of a donkey in length but shorter legged, with a tail as long as its body.' He and his colleagues were in their fishing boat at the time and watched it for 20 minutes, clearly visible against the white cliffs, as it jumped two crevasses before disappearing over the cliff top.

Jim Miller and his crew watched a black panther jumping small crevasses on the white cliffs in the 1960s

Coombe Keynes to Lulworth Camp – March 2002

The witness, Neil, wrote: 'Back in 2002 I was working as a vehicle engineer at Lulworth Camp. I was living at Bovington at that time. It was early one March morning, if my memory serves me right a Tuesday, at approximately 6.40 a.m. I was riding my push bike to Lulworth south along the B3071 and decided to push my bike the last hundred metres up the hill. As I got half way I noticed to my left a low-lying tree in a boundary hedge, approximately 8 m away from me. The tree had a low-lying, thick branch, about 3.5 m long that came off the tree horizontally towards the road. The reason I was alerted to this tree was because … this sounds daft but I felt something watching me, and as I stood and looked in speechless amazement, there in front of me on the branch was lying a large black cat, which I can only describe as looking like a panther. It was looking at me, and then with no great urgency it pushed itself off the branch and down on to the ground into the field behind bushes, and that was the last I saw of this wonderful, powerful-looking creature. When I got to work I told several of my friends about what I had seen and they laughed at me. So from then on I was very shy to tell anyone of my experience. I don't think there has been a day goes by over the last 5 years when I haven't thought about what I can only describe as a wonderful experience.'

Flower's Barrow, Lulworth Ranges – 10 April 2004

On Saturday 10 April a London woman and her husband, experienced walkers and used to observing the local fauna, were hiking in the Lulworth Ranges and she described the following experience: 'Between 7 and 7.30 p.m. (i.e. before sunset) my husband and I saw a large black feline-looking creature on one of the Lulworth Range walks. We were heading east on the trail up to Flower's Barrow, and we saw the creature roughly 150 yards away, on the hill horizon, slightly to the left of the path, to the north. The hill horizon was not the final crest of Flower's Barrow, but one of the 'false horizons' on the way up. Our glimpse was very brief; it was the movement of its running into a thicket of brush to the north that caught our attention. It was long enough for me to tell my husband to look where I pointed, and for him to get a reasonable look, as it ran along, but not long enough for us to think of getting out our binoculars. How long is that? I don't really know – but not long, probably much less than a minute. The creature was totally black. It ran somewhat low to the ground, in a streak, moving very fast and in an entirely straight line. We did not notice a tail one way or another. My husband puts its size as 'below the knee', the size of a large lamb. I thought it might have been a bit bigger, somewhere between lamb and Labrador, but I think it was difficult to tell the height exactly as it had the impression of racing low to the ground. Its coat seemed to be more smooth than long or rough. It was more lynx size than panther or mountain lion size – but it was black, which I don't think is a typical lynx thing, and the body shape seemed lower to the ground, but I'm not really familiar with how lynx run. We both thought that by the way it moved it was very definitely not a dog and very definitely not a lamb, and very feline. I would describe this movement quality as having something to do with the fluidity of movement in the rear haunch, and the ability to go at a lickety split race pace, while remaining low to the ground. We are very sure it was a cat-type thing, based on the movement quality.

There was nobody else about on the range walks that we could see, at that point, and it was very quiet. Previously we had seen hikers heading for the campground at Lulworth, when we were resting at Arish Mell, and afterwards, at Worbarrow Bay we saw a kayaker camping in a tunnel tent and a few people fishing. But at that time we were the only people in sight. We were not making any special effort to be quiet on the trail, but we were not being very noisy either. I have a Leki hiking stick which makes a click, and it might have been that that alerted the animal. I had the impression that it was racing for cover, rather than attacking or just running for no particular reason. We stared at each other in a kind of extended eyebrow-raised "Did you see what I saw?" kind of double take. We stayed still for a while to see if there was anything else to see, or if it made a further move. I wasn't really concerned for our safety as the animal was clearly trying to get out of sight, and wasn't directly in our path. But nonetheless I did look around me afterwards quite often, as did my husband.'

East Lulworth – August 2005

The witness wrote: 'I live in East Lulworth and see a lot of deer and wild animals whilst walking. One morning in early August 2005 I was passing the old garage heading out for a day's fishing when something in a side road leading to the East Lulworth bypass caught my eye, so I stopped to have a look. It was an animal about the height of a Labrador but a lot longer and it had a long curled tail and a very muscular build. It stood in the middle of the road just looking at me, then just walked into the hedgerow out of sight. I was about 25 ft from it, but it did not seem concerned by my presence and was in no real hurry. I also sighted another creature of about the same size but dark grey in colour about 2 months later in the field directly behind my house late in the evening just before dark.'

Belhuish, Coombe Keynes – 31 November 2006

Leslie Burt reported: 'It was at Belhuish – my birthplace. It was supposed once to have been occupied by monks and I get the feeling they left something behind. I was making my annual pilgrimage there because it was my birthday. It's my spiritual home you might say. It's part of the Weld estate and my grandfather lived there and worked as a gamekeeper. My parents lived there, as well as uncles, aunts, cousins. I was one of 30 grandchildren. It was November – a cold day. I was waiting for my daughter to come and collect me. It was shaded down at the farm, so I walked up the hill purposely to get into the sun. As I was walking, facing up the hill, I distinctly saw this big sleek black cat – the size of a fat greyhound. Quite a size. It walked slowly across the lane, right to left, from one hedge to the other. Then it came slowly back again the way it had come, but this time saw me and stopped for a moment and looked at me. It was not a domestic cat or dog; it was something

Leslie Burt saw a black panther-like animal cross this path near Lulworth

entirely different. It was so close I couldn't mistake it – about 40 yards. It was so quiet you could have heard a pin drop.'

🐾 Lyme Regis

30 April 1995
A 'large feline animal' was reportedly seen near Lyme Regis, and again in 1997, worrying sheep.

Colway Lane – 12 September 1995
The *Dorset Echo* reported: 'Experienced countryman and nature watcher Cecil Quick saw a panther-like animal in a field near his Lyme Regis home, off Colway Lane, and is one of several people who have reported sightings recently. Mr Quick, who breeds pheasants and hunts with his own gun dogs, added: "It is definitely not a domestic animal. I have never before seen anything like it." The mystery beast has been seen on several occasions in the Sleechwood and Pen Cross areas of Lyme Regis and in the Bridport area.'

Raymond's Hill – 9 May 1997
The *Bridport and Lyme Regis News* reported: 'Photographer Richard Austin of Lyme Regis was up at Raymond's Hill capturing snow pictures on Tuesday. He had focused his lens on a rabbit crouched under a snowy buttercup when he saw a black shape in the corner of the frame. "I thought it was a dog at first along by the hedge, and I thought, 'Oh no, he's going to see me and start barking'. But then I looked again and realised it was a big cat. It was absolutely jet black; so black that when it turned its head towards me you couldn't make out its features – they just blended in. It turned sideways and I just managed to bang off a couple of frames before it leapt though the hedge and disappeared." Disappointingly, the pictures turned out to be unusable.'

● SHOCK FOR PHOTOGRAPHER AS HE FOCUSES LENS AND SEES LARGE BLACK CAT

Snapper's brush with black beast in snow

Story by SARA HUDSTON

A BRUSH with what could be the black beast of Broadwindsor left photographer Richard Austin shaking with surprise this week.

black that when it turned its head towards me you couldn't

near his home in West Milton.

He said: "It was far too big to be a domestic cat — it was definitely a big cat."

Stuart saw the animal in a

Those who have seen the beast describe it as a puma or panther-like animal about the size of a large dog.

From Bridport and Lyme Regis News report by Sara Hudston

River Lim, Uplyme – 2 May 2004

It was a warm, sunny day, sometime between 4 and 7 p.m. Andy Finlay and Alison Ludlam were out walking from Uplyme to Lyme Regis along the public footpath that hugs the River Lim. Andy reported: 'There is a field next to the river with a lot of sheep and lambs in it; it also has families of wild rabbits. We were stopped, looking at the lambs and the small rabbits, when I said to Alison, "Look at the size of that dog, it moves like a cat!" It was trotting diagonally down the hillside; very fast, very close to the ground, not stalking the way a domestic cat does, but moving very quickly. It came to within 50 m of us when it noticed us and – upon seeing us – it turned 90 degrees without stopping, and disappeared into some cover behind some bushes at the edge of the field. We stood still hoping to see a further glimpse of whatever it was. But nothing, though we waited for about 15 minutes. I figured it was more scared of us than we of it. It was a very dark brown, but this colour was not uniform across the body, there were lighter patches of fur. The length of its body was about 5–6 ft and the length of the tail about 2 ft.'

🐾 Lytchett Matravers

6 December 2005

At 3.15 p.m. a black panther-like animal was reported at Lytchett Matravers. It was in a field adjacent to Middle Road on the outskirts of the village.

20 January 2006

Tom Tryon emailed Richard Hammond's 5 O'Clock television show after a feature on big cats: 'I have seen a lynx on multiple occasions in Lytchett Matravers, Dorset. Other members of my family have also seen it and our dog (a Jack Russell) even scared it away.'

🐾 Maiden Newton

1960s

Mike Davis recalled seeing a big cat at Maiden Newton more than four decades ago: 'It amazes me that I hadn't remembered this till now … . But I had a girlfriend in Maiden Newton for years, when I was a teenager. I'm 60 now so that would have been about 1960. We used to go up into the countryside to do some courting. Her father, Mr Stone, worked on the railways and said, "Don't go up there" – I think it's called Narn Hill – "there's a big cat up there." I said, "What do you mean?" and he said "There it is now" – and pointed it out to me on the hillside. We never went up there after that. Mr Stone said that the people that owned the hillside land had brought it back to England.' Note – Narn Hill is the local name for Norden Hill.

2002/2003 and 2007/2008

Ray O'Donovan saw a black big cat 'just walking across a field. It was black with a long tail, and bigger than a fox.' About the same time, Richard Smith took a video of what looked like a black panther-type cat on the hill the far side of the railway line onto which the housing estate backs.

Andy Elliott, a Countryside Ranger, often saw it on this hillside, 'especially on still sunny afternoons'. On one occasion he filmed it, and a fox passed in the foreground, providing a useful scale of size for the animal. Andy wrote: 'I have lived in West Dorset all my life and worked here as a Countryside Ranger for 18 years. During this time many people have spoken to me of big cat sightings or asked me 'Do you think I could have seen … ?' Many of them described cat-like creatures that fell into two descriptive types: black leopard or lynx. These sightings were over a large area of West Dorset including Batcombe Down, Minterne Magna, Eggardon Hill, Beaminster and Maiden Newton. I was sceptical at first but many of the witnesses were people that I considered reliable and indeed they were as sceptical as I was even after their sighting. I then had my own first glimpse of what I could only describe as a big cat. This was between Batcombe Down and Minterne Magna. I saw a tall brown cat that is best described as lynx-like moving along a roadside ditch. I stopped my Land Rover in an attempt to get a better view but without success. I was still not convinced but could not categorise it in any other way.

During 2002/2003 I regularly started to see a large black cat on the hills above Maiden Newton. It would lie in the sun on warm evenings. A number of other people also saw it around the same time and asked me what it might be. Some of them were quite embarrassed about asking as they thought I would simply dismiss them as fools. They were reassured that their sighting was of a big cat, though I couldn't identify it beyond a big black leopard-type cat. I saw it many times and twice observed it with a fox. The first time they came almost nose to nose, checked each other out, then the fox moved away. Neither was particularly disturbed by the experience. The cat was slightly larger than the fox and its tail was distinctly different, long and evenly broad. The second time I was with a group of friends and we were watching the cat on the hill. When I saw the fox approach I thought it was worth trying to capture this on video. The fox walked past the cat, possibly not even being aware that the cat was there because the cat sank into the grass out of view. When the fox had passed, the cat popped its head back up to take a look around, then it got up and moved off into cover. The date was the 16th March 2003 and it was the last sighting that I had of that particular cat.

In the last couple of years (2007/2008) people have again been reporting cat sightings to me so it may well have returned to the area, though I have not seen it myself.'

Whitesheet Hill – May 2003

John Earl was driving on the road to Crewkerne at about 6 a.m. one morning in May. About a mile beyond Maiden Newton, at the top of the hill, he was surprised to see what was unmistakably a big cat emerge from the hedge on the right and cross the road less than 50 yards in front of him. He said: 'It was amazing to see. It was dark in colour, though not black, and about the size of an Alsatian bitch. It had cat's ears, sticking up, but I did not notice its tail'. Two weeks later, at about the same time of day and in exactly the same place, he saw the animal again. This time the mystery feline emerged from the left-hand hedge, reached the middle of the road, looked at him, turned and retreated the way it had come. Being high up in a van he once again got a very good look at it. He said: 'It just sauntered slowly; it was in no hurry at all – lovely to see'. Searching in a book of big cats subsequently he felt that a picture of a European lynx bore the closest resemblance to the animal he had seen. One of the reasons for this was that he felt that if the animal had had a long tail, as other big cats do, he would have noticed it.

Wynford Eagle – March 2007

Virginia Astley and Catherine Simmonds had gone for a walk on the old railway line to Toller Fratrum. Virginia recalled: 'We were coming from Wynford Eagle to Maiden Newton, and half way along on the left-hand side there is a barn. We saw an animal – the top of it, then it vanished. The thought that it could be a deer or fox obviously crossed our minds, and Catherine has always lived in the country and is familiar with these animals. Then we saw it completely, going towards a gate. It was bizarre; a very orangey colour, too big for a domestic cat – a big dog size. It looked like a kind of toy, so completely not like anything I'd ever seen – a small orange lion. It was in a field with a stream to the left, on the far side of the stream, about 100 m away, walking along parallel with us. It then vanished out of view and a rabbit came tearing across the field towards us. I didn't notice much of a tail. It had a strange shaped head, quite fluffyish. Just wasn't like anything. We were so mystified and wondered if it was some kind of odd pet. The colour was almost unreal. If either of us had been alone we would have thought we had imagined it.'

The road from Wynford Eagle to Maiden Newton

🐾 Mannington

Mannington, Horton, Holt, Row Common and Uddens – Summer 2005

Ben House wrote: 'I am from Dorset originally and my parents still live in the county, in a small hamlet called Mannington, not far from Wimborne Minster. Since about 2000 there has been talk of a big cat being occasionally sighted in that general area.

In summer 2005 a family was camping in the field that backs onto my parents' field.

One day, at about 2.00 p.m. they apparently witnessed an anomalous big cat walk the length of my parents' field. I think they described it as either panther- or puma-like. Whatever the animal was, they promptly packed away their tent and fled! This was told to me on one of my visits home, roughly a week after the event.

Interestingly there is a well-known local legend about a ghostly black dog, which haunts the road by Horton (Queens) Copse. Horton Copse is part of a large area of woodland that merges into Holt Forest. The part nearest the Horton road is known as Queens Copse. It lies roughly half way between Three Legged Cross and Horton village, on the Horton road. I think it's the stretch of road that passes the Drusillas Inn that the dog is supposed to haunt. I don't know of anyone who has actually ever seen the black dog, but it was definitely a story that I was told when I was little. My Dad reckons (sceptically) that stories of black dogs were made up by smugglers to keep people off the roads at night! The location of the big cat sighting (Mannington) is roughly a mile away from Queens Copse.

I think I also remember someone saying it had been seen on Row Common, and also at Uddens. I'm afraid that I don't have any first-hand stories though, and none of my family has sighted it … yet!'

❧ Martinstown

1990 onwards

A witness wrote: 'My first sighting was when I was younger; however, I distinctly remember it. Me and two friends were playing army and I looked at some woods and saw a black big cat gliding along the outskirts of a small wood, with birds circling and dive-bombing it from high up. I saw this cat through binoculars from about 50 m and could make it out clearly before alerting my friends.

The next time, I was rough shooting with my friends with a rifle and we saw a black figure crouched on a wall next to a field of sheep. It had pointed ears and a long tail curving towards the ground. We watched it for around 10 minutes through the rifle scope. I am unsure about how tall it was, but I would estimate maybe 1.25 m. I fired the rifle and the figure ran off. This creature was the wrong shape for a dog and moved in a very different way. My friend I was with saw this also. A teacher at school once told me that in the same area he once saw out of the corner of his eye, quite closely, a black figure run into undergrowth and then a rabbit jumping out and running from the undergrowth. My father claims once after a few drinks to have seen a lioness in front of the car with a friend.'

❧ Melcombe Bingham

Various sightings of big cats have been reported from this area, though not much detail is available. Anne Beckett saw a black cat at Higher Ansty; another was spotted in a garden near Cliff Wood. The Head of Milton Abbas School is reputed to have glimpsed a big cat, 'and another crossed the road in front of a car in pouring rain'.

July 2004

Anne and Alan Stevens heard a racket in their garden and saw a roe deer hung up on a fence with its guts torn out – they heard growling from a bush and saw a cat's face within it.

🐾 Melplash

North west from the Cricket Club – 1995

Simon Beal had been playing cricket at Melplash and they had been rained off for a while. While he and his friends sat in the changing room they looked across in the Broadwindsor direction and saw a dark, cat-like figure ambling down a field following the fence line. The size of the animal arrested their attention, said Simon, 'and we watched it for quite a little while'. It was about 4 ft long and 2 ft high. Simon shoots and is used to seeing the native fauna, 'but this wasn't an animal I recognised'.

31 January 2004

There was another sighting of the mystery big cat following a story in the *Bridport and Lyme Regis News* the previous week. The newspaper reported: 'Liz Jones, wife of Tote chairman Peter Jones, saw the creature at Melplash on Saturday at about midday. "I was looking out of my mother's kitchen window towards the garden in our farmyard," she said. "I was amazed to see a very black animal appear from behind a low privet hedge about 30 yards from the house." At first Mrs Jones thought it was a calf, but as it jumped over the hedge she noticed in particular that the creature had a very long, cat-like tail curving upwards. "It jumped down the bank and out of view behind a wall," she said. "When I turned to look out of a window on the other side of the room I saw it at the bottom of our drive heading towards the road that runs through Melplash, the A3066. It was fairly close to the ground. It all happened so quickly and briefly that I cannot be sure what it was, but the tail was very distinctive. It was much too big to be a domestic cat, and very black." Mrs Jones is convinced that what she saw was not a black dog. "It was the way it carried the tail and the way it 'flowed' over the hedge and low wall and also left no footprints in the rain-softened low bank, which it would have done had it been any farm animal," she said. "Wild boar was what I thought when it went down the drive because it was low to the ground and they have recently escaped, but the tail and the blackness just stick in my memory."'

25 February 2005

The *Bridport News* reported: 'This time it was by Wendy and Richard Plummer of Slades Green, Bridport, who were driving on the Beaminster road on Saturday morning when they saw the black panther-like animal. Mrs Plummer said: "We were driving to Beaminster and in Melplash we had just turned the corner up the hill when I looked through a gap in the hedge and there it was two fields away. There was nothing else in the field. It was 11.35 a.m., the sun was out and it was slinking, like a cat does, hunching its shoulders. It was definitely a big cat. Had it been a normal cat we would not have seen it two fields away."'

🐾 Merley

April 1999

The local press reported: 'In April, a taxi driver contacted police after he spotted a large, lean-looking beast roaming woodland near Merley, fuelling speculation that an animal previously spotted in the area may have returned.'

🐾 Milton Abbas

Milton Abbas and Bryanston Schools – July 2004

The *Dorset Echo* reported: 'A big cat has been reported roaming the north Dorset countryside near two schools. The creature has been described as being similar to a leopard in appearance and size and was seen late at night and in the early hours of the morning in three locations around the county this month. Dorset Police have received three reports of the big cat in just over a week. It was first sighted close to Milton Abbas Primary School at around 11 p.m. on July 7, then Bryanston School at 3 a.m. on July 8, before being spotted in the back garden of a house in Nether Compton at around 4.20 a.m. on July 15. PC John Snellin, wildlife officer for Dorset Police, said: "A big cat of similar appearance has been spotted a couple of times around the Verwood area. It is described as looking like a black leopard and is quite distinctive. Compared with the number of sightings we usually get, this has been quite an increase. Until now it has been a very quiet few months. It could be that the good weather is drawing them to the area, but there doesn't seem to be any particular reason for its presence apart from that. Maybe people were more inclined to report the sightings to police because of the close proximity to schools. But I would assure people it's no great cause for concern – big cats tend to stay out of people's way."'

🐾 Mockbeggar (Hampshire border)

South Gorley Road – August 2006

Jonathan McGowan reported: 'Barry Collier saw a large spotted cat cross the road in front of him during the night at 10.30 p.m. and enter the opposite hedge along a well-worn run. The sighting was between South Gorley and Mockbeggar. The cat's body was blotched dark and yellow with spots merging into stripes. It was the size of a Labrador, but taller and longer – long thin tail. After looking at the internet for pictures of cats he is convinced the animal he saw was an ocelot.'

🐾 Monkton Wyld

18 September 2005

Rose Luckman wrote: 'I thought I'd get in touch because I saw an animal that looked like a big cat earlier this evening. When I got home I was met with scepticism, so I looked up Dorset big cats on the internet and found your website. I was driving home to Monkton Wyld from working at Tesco in Axminster about 5.15 this evening. There were road works in Axminster so I couldn't take my usual route. I took another route which I don't know very well towards the A35, aiming for the turn-off to the west of the one I usually take. I had never actually driven this way before, and I missed the turning. I carried on until I found a small road where I could turn the car round. As I turned into it, I saw a man and an animal further up the road. At first glance it looked like a man taking a dog for a walk. Then I saw that it wasn't a dog. It was difficult to see exactly what colour it was, because the light was behind it, but I think it had some kind of pattern in its coat, maybe stripes, and it seemed to be a dark greyish or brownish colour. I could see its shape quite clearly, and there is no other way to describe it except as a very large cat. It was about the size of a small to medium size dog. Then it turned and walked into the hedge. I ran through the possibilities in my mind … dog … fox … deer … but it was the wrong shape for any of them. It wasn't a badger either, it was definitely cat-shaped. I turned to the friend I was with, and said "What was that? It looked like a very big cat". He said, "Maybe he's got the kind of cat you take for walks". But then we decided that the man probably wasn't taking it for a walk, because of the way it disappeared into the hedge. He seemed to be just looking at it.

When I got back home I mentioned over dinner that I had seen an exceptionally large cat, and immediately people started talking about urban legends, myths, ghosts and so forth. Until then I had not connected what I had seen with reports of big cats in the media. I'm rather reluctant to report it to the police, as suggested on the *BBC News* website (Warning after 'Big Cat' sighting, 24 August 2005) because it didn't seem to be doing any harm, and wasn't at all frightening – it was just walking along quite slowly, first along the road and then into the hedge, in the way that animals do around here … . It seems a bit unnecessary to hunt it down. However, I did think that it was worth informing you about it.'

🐾 Mosterton

River Axe – 25 June 2006

Catherine and Mark Jones saw a black or dark, long, low, cat-like creature in the shallow valley where the River Axe runs between Mosterton and Seaborough: 'We saw it across one field and it was half way across the next, about 60 yards from the river. We often watch the foxes in that field, and it was not in the slightest bit fox-like! I suspect it was hunting from the way it was moving (we have cats and it was very similar). We watched it for about 2 minutes, and then it passed through a hedge into woodland. Unfortunately the batteries in my camera were not charged (typical!).'

🐾 Motcombe

1994

This summer saw several appearances of the 'Motcombe Beast', as the newspapers dubbed it. Loud yowling noises were also heard over several months, and 3-inch feline paw prints were discovered near the home of Mr and Mrs Talbot. About ten sightings were reported from East Stour and Motcombe, several by lifelong country folk familiar with wildlife. Marcus Matthews, who lives in Wiltshire and has been collecting big cat sightings for several decades, reported the following:

'In 1994 a large tawny cat similar to a jungle cat was sighted at Motcombe Hill, near Shaftesbury. It crossed the road quickly.'

'One farmer saw the cat twice on Motcombe Hill and thought it resembled a puma. Another farmer, finding a roe deer in the woods dying from bites to its throat, went to his Land Rover for a shotgun to put it out of its misery. When he returned the deer had gone and he glimpsed an animal through the undergrowth. He believed it to have been a big cat. He also heard a high-pitched, cat-like scream and his dog shook with fear.'

'Another man saw a large black cat in daylight in the churchyard at East Stour. It was also seen crossing a field by two men who were interviewed in Motcombe village by Meridian Television News.'

'A couple who owned a cattery saw a lynx-like cat several times and photographed a paw print over a muddy drain, which was published at the time in the *Blackmoor Vale Magazine* and the *Western Daily Press*.'

🐾 Netherbury

29 September 2000

The *Bridport News* reported: 'Market trader Eric Fox of Melksham, Wiltshire, had stopped in a lay-by on the A3066 Bridport to Beaminster road near Netherbury at around 7 a.m. when he saw a huge black cat moving over the bank. "I opened the car door and this thing came up over the bank. I thought, 'Oh Christ, it's coming towards me' and I just froze. I didn't move. If I had moved I think it would have gone for me. It was carrying something in its mouth – it must have been a dog or a fox. … It stalked directly across the road in front of my car and on to the other side of the road. It was brown or black in colour and between 4 and 5 ft long, 2 ft high with a tail about 2 ft long." Mr Fox, who runs a china and glass stall, believes he may have seen the "beast" before and in the same area of Dorset. "I wasn't sure what it was the first time;

I thought it was a shadow." After this encounter he rang the Bridport Police to inform them of the incident.'

July 2001
Max Dack is from Seaton in Devon. One fine July day in 2001 he and his wife decided to go for a cycle ride, from Bridport to Beaminster. They had gone up a lane, through Waytown, and had a drink and picnic at Netherbury, then looked at the church and strolled around the village. Max knew Parnham House was between Netherbury and Beaminster, and so when he saw a path leading towards the brow of a hill he thought he'd go up it to see if there was a view of the big house below. They crossed a stream, and went up the cart track through a field of corn, heading for the brow, hoping to see Parnham House beyond it. 'All of a sudden this thing walked out across the track 40 ft in front of me – and totally ignored me. It was the size of an Alsatian dog or a Labrador, and as black as the ace of spades. Its tail was enormous – thick and large, and coming right down to the ground. It was absolutely beautiful and in pristine condition – so confident, so healthy. It crossed the 12-ft-wide track and went into the corn the other side. It was funny that it didn't turn to look at us; its complete distain unnerved me. We saw nothing more and continued up the track to the brow of the hill, but couldn't see Parnham House, and so returned the way we had come. … I rang the police. But it was a beautiful, beautiful thing. I was gob smacked.'

September 2003
Sixteen-year-old Ashley Blanning from Bridport saw the beast on his way to work as an apprentice on a Beaminster farm in September 2003. He was riding his moped near the Netherbury turning on the Crooked Oak bends when he saw the animal running down the field on his right. His mother, Kim, said: 'He is certain it was a cat. He pulled in and tried to ring me but couldn't get a signal. It was black and had a huge tail that was literally being dragged on the ground. He's never seen anything like it. Ashley said it was going at such a speed; it was such a powerful animal. He said you had to see it to believe it.'

27 January 2004
The *Dorset Echo* reported: 'The big black cat roaming West Dorset has been spotted again. It was seen by Margery Hookings, editor of the *Echo's* sister paper the *Bridport News*, as she was driving on the A3066 road between Melplash and Beaminster. She saw a black, panther-like animal about 400 yards away on hills near the Netherbury turning. The location is the same as a previous sighting by teenager Ashley Blanning, from Bridport, who witnessed a similar animal running down the field in September on his way to work on a Beaminster farm. Margery said: "It was about 4.45 p.m. but still daylight. I was rounding the bend near the first Netherbury turning when I looked out across the sloping fields to my left. I saw the distinct shape of a big cat sauntering down the hill towards the hedge. I estimate it was about the size of my dog – an English Setter – but leaner, longer and closer to the ground. What struck me was that it was very black, like a silhouette, and had a very long tail. I couldn't pull in because I had a car behind me, but I looked back and saw it was still there, making its way down to the

hedge." She added: "I certainly felt very privileged to see it and have no doubts about what I saw."'

Margery Hookings' black feline animal (see above) was also seen in the same location by Malcolm Dewar of Gerrards Green, Beaminster. He reported: 'On 27 January I was driving towards Beaminster with my wife at 4.45 p.m. when I saw a big cat in a field at Melplash near the Netherbury road. I said, "Look over there" to my wife, Pauline, and pointed at the big cat and she saw it as well. It looked just like a fully grown puma walking close to the hedgerow. It was 4–5 ft long, very black, with a long curved tail. It must have been in view for about 15 seconds. It was just ambling along by the hedge quietly, maybe sniffing around for a rabbit or rodent to eat.'

28 March 2004

David Wakely was driving home to Beaminster from Bridport, and at the first Netherbury turn, near Melplash, he spotted a jet-black feline animal coming down the field: 'I thought, "There's that black cat" – and watched it as it came down from the top of the hill. It was approximately 250–300 yards away, and about the size of a small Alsatian dog. I've lived here all my life and never seen it before.' His son had seen a similar animal 2 years previously at Salway Ash.

The first Netherbury turn after Melplash, where several witnesses spotted a big black cat

4 April 2004

A Bridport man driving on the A3066 between Bridport and Melplash, at about 2 p.m., stopped when he was alerted by another motorist, who had stopped her car on sight of a large black cat. He wrote: 'I saw the cat too and can confirm it was a black cat, heavy build, large dog size but short legged. We were about 150–200 yards away from the animal and it was walking across an orchard. As we approached, it calmly and slowly disappeared into the hedgerow and into the next field and away.'

Parnham House – July 2005

Mrs Susan Tinklin wrote: 'I have just been reading your report on the animal sighted near Netherbury. My friend saw a big black cat also, just outside Parnham House, just off the turning to Netherbury. He said it was a very big animal, and having travelled a lot this man knows what he saw. My husband and I went and took some photos near the spot, and found a paw print bigger than a 50 pence piece. As you are collecting sightings I thought you should know.'

26 March 2007

Hannah Bareham wrote: 'I thought I should e-mail about a recent sighting of a big cat in Netherbury. I was surprised, after reading some of the previous sightings, that our experience matched others in so many ways. I was driving from Bridport and took the first turning into Netherbury after Melplash. There were three of us in the car and just as we dropped down from the main road we saw a very large black cat cross the road and walk through the hedge into the field to the right. It was about the size of a small Labrador but carried itself low to the ground. It wasn't in a hurry and just casually walked through the hedge. We slowed right down to allow it to move out of the road, but we didn't stop the car as it had disappeared into the hedgerow. It didn't seem to take any notice of the car, and it didn't turn to us so I didn't see its face or notice its ears. It took its time and didn't seem frightened of the car. What really struck me was the size and length of its tail – very thick and heavy and it seemed to hang down to the ground, close to the animal's body and then curl up again at the end. This encounter is so similar to some of the others – same place and same description; I just thought you'd be interested to know about it.'

🐾 Nether Compton

15 July 2004

A large, black, leopard-like cat was spotted in a back garden of a house at Nether Compton at approximately 4.20 a.m.

🐾 Osmington

Osmington Mills – 13 June 2004

A witness from Bristol reported the following sighting: 'On Sunday June 13th I was walking with my 16-year-old son from Osmington Mills to Spring Bottom along the footpath. It was 10 a.m. We were walking past a field on our left when I noticed an animal's head raised above the crop. It was lying down, and it was a large cat. I pointed it out to my son. The cat turned to look at us, but it did not seem alarmed by us. I took out my camera, but because it was only a disposable type the animal was out of viewing range. I walked into the field to get closer for a picture, and the cat looked around again and slowly started to crawl on its belly (dragging itself with its front legs) up the field away from me until it disappeared into the crop.

We spotted it again a minute or so later further up the field still crawling. The cat was a light brown/fawn colour all over (as much as I could see). It had a longish tail and noticeable ears. They were stuck up, and as it turned I could see the pink tinge inside. I estimate the cat's body was between 2 ft and 30 inches long; the colour and shape reminded me of a miniature lioness.'

7 February 2006

The *Dorset Echo* reported: 'Following numerous sightings of a lynx-like creature in the Westham area of Weymouth last year (2005) the Dorset Police log has become active again with the news from Osmington of "a big white cat the size of a large Labrador". Apparently a driver spied it in his rear-view mirror one afternoon. "Calls like this are treated seriously and we urge people to contact us with future sightings", one officer helpfully suggests.'

🐾 Owermoigne

24 February 2006

Ralph Cree wrote: 'My wife and I saw a large black cat run across a field at dusk, in Owermoigne about 3 weeks ago. It looked about half the size of a deer – because it ran right past some. The local farmer has seen it, and photographed it as well.'

18 July 2006

Dave Dennett reported: 'Hi, I saw a cat today at about 4.30 p.m. I was sat in the garden of my sister's house, which is 5 miles west of Wool on the Dorchester Road, looking across a field, when something caught my eye. At first I thought it was just a domestic cat … but as it walked across the field I noticed three very different things about it. The way it walked was so different from a normal domestic cat. It had very large ears indeed (pricked up). It was so amazingly long. It was some 20–30 m away. The colour was a dark brown to a very dark brown (forgive me, the sun was behind it so I can't be more specific). However, when it saw me it stopped, froze, then sat down. That is when I really noticed the ears … almost triangular, but long. I called my sister and we both studied it; she was concerned immediately. It stood up and walked, not like a normal cat but very slow and laboriously, with a very long body indeed and a smooth curved tail.'

🐾 Piddletrenthide

Rockpits Farm, Plush – 14 November 2000

The *Dorset Echo* reported: 'A black panther-like creature has been spotted roaming farmland north of Dorchester by two people. The mysterious animal was first sighted by Pauline Perks outside her kitchen window and then again by her husband Jeffrey.

And the couple's description of the black beast is similar to that of an animal seen on Portland last week. Mr and Mrs Perks live at Rockpits Farm in Plush, a village outside Dorchester. Mrs Perks, 47, a housewife, said: "I saw the creature 3 or 4 weeks ago, but when I read in the Echo that something just the same had been seen on Portland, I got in touch with the police. It was right outside my kitchen window. It just shot straight past and I saw it as plain as can be. It was absolutely black and as big as an Alsatian dog. It had its ears sticking back, flat on its head. I've got two Labrador dogs, one golden and one black, but it definitely wasn't the dogs. It was a big cat, like the black panthers you see in the zoo. I told my husband and he said I was going mad, but then a few days later he was up at the barn behind the house and he, too, came face to face with it.'"

*From Dorset Echo report
by Joanna Quinn*

THE YEAR OF THE CAT: Pauline Perks stands near the trees where she saw the puma-like cat from her farm's kitchen window   (EJT)

Dole's Ash Plantation – 11 September 2006

A witness wrote: 'I saw a big cat today. If you were to ask me what kind of cat it was I would have to say that it looked like a female lion or a young male lion. But I'm no expert and I do not want publicity.

I took a late afternoon/early evening walk from Piddlehinton to Dole's Ash Plantation. On the way back I stopped by a gate into a field almost opposite the turning to Bourne Farm where the road turns into a track. As I looked across the field I saw what I first thought to be a deer watching me. The animal then bounded a few metres to get into longer grass where it stopped, crouched down and popped its head above the grass and was watching me. It was about 150 m away. When it moved I realised immediately that it was not a deer. It was big and long with a long tail and it leapt like a cat. It had strong back quarters and strong front quarters that were powerful. It was a sandy-brown colour, but parts of it were darker brown. In some ways it looked like a giant fox, but it was much bigger than any fox or dog. It was big! It sat watching me with its head above the grass. From the front its head was oblong, but it had a whiter triangular face that made it look like an upturned whitish triangle. It did not seem to have pointed ears. I was a long way from any habitation and I can tell you I was worried.

Then I noticed a big stag in the corner of the field. The stag was also stood watching the animal. The stag came cautiously into the field and when the animal noticed it the stag charged at it. A stag would never charge at a fox or dog when it was in the open field well away from any other deer ... When the stag charged the animal I saw the full size of it. Although I was some distance away it was big, very big. It had a very big long tail and it ran quickly in a leaping motion. Not like a dog. Again it was fox-like but huge and powerful. It ran out of sight over the brow of the hill, towards the general direction that I had to walk.

When I got to my car which was parked near the Grain Mill I had a good look around. I drove to a farm to see if there were any big dogs around. The farm did have a very big kennel. Perhaps it was a really big dog, but I genuinely don't think so. The animal was about as tall as a Great Dane, for example, but it was much longer than any dog I have ever seen and it didn't run like a dog. More like a giant – and I mean giant – fox. It also had a big oblong face that was largely white. To me, and I am not joking, it looked like a lion.'

The witness subsequently searched on the internet for a match with the animal he saw, and sent a photo of a puma: 'I have been trying to find pictures of what I saw today and although this is a close up this is the animal that I saw. Quite definitely. This is the face that was looking at me, the body shape and the powerful muscles.'

White Lackington Drove – October 2007

Emma Hawkes again saw what seemed to be the puma-like animal she had seen the previous year (see Charlton Down, 13 July 2006): 'I did see the cat again; however, it was getting dark and it was really too far away to be definite. It was on a hillside below White Lackington Drove. I was on the hill in the valley opposite and had no binoculars, but its behaviour was unusual for a deer as it stalked from bush to bush out of my view each time I moved to get a better view. I had it in view for about 15 minutes until it sloped back up the hill into the undergrowth.

🐾 Portland, Isle of

Easton – September 1995

A big cat was reportedly seen at a quarry in Easton in September 1995, but there are no further details available.

Victoria Place – 29 September 1995

The *Dorset Echo* reported: 'Mr Ken Lewington of Easton was walking his dog around the rough land in the vicinity of the old coal yard at the end of Victoria Place. "While walking up one of the inclines, I happened to glance back and saw this creature not 50 yards behind me but walking away from me. I was close enough to see it was a long, black/grey animal with a shoulder height of approximately 18 inches, and it was moving in a feline fashion with its large tail swishing."'

Grove Road allotments – 23 February 1996

The *Dorset Echo* again reported: 'Spending half term with relatives on the island, schoolteacher Mr Jack Dews from Wakefield thought his eyes were playing tricks when

From Dorset Echo report

he spotted a creature, much larger than a domestic cat, sunning itself on the cliff face alongside the Grove Road allotments. Mr Dews said: "I was amazed to spot this lynx-like animal which had a flat face, was smooth-furred and a dark grey striped colour. I have never seen anything like it before and I reckon it was about 2 ft long." He added: "It sat tall on a rock, unmoving but watching closely as I stood there with my sister-in-law's dog.'"

The Weares – 1999

In the area of the Weares in June 1999 many islanders saw a strange feline about the size of a spaniel, and dark tabby in colour.

Church Ope Cove – 9 November 2000

The local press reported: 'Police swooped on Church Ope Cove, Portland, after a call from a worried member of the public. The caller told police he had seen a black cat "about the size of an Alsatian" near a cliff as he walked towards the cove. Acting Sergeant Jamie Clark of Portland Police was called to the scene to investigate. He said: "We've no doubt about the authenticity of the call. A man who lives in the area rang us after spotting what he described as a large black cat near the cliff. He said it was about 50 yards away from where he stood and was about the size of an Alsatian dog." Acting Sgt Clark added: "I checked out the area but was unable to find anything. We certainly haven't had any reports of escaped animals in the area."'

Tout Quarry – 16 February 2004

Mrs W wrote: 'On Monday 16th February 2004, my friend and I were visiting Tout Quarry in Portland when to our amazement, and initial disbelief, we spotted a large black cat, about as big as a fox. It was approximately 20 ft away from us and in sight for about 10 seconds. It had a very long thin tail, approximately one-and-a-half times its body length, curling up at the end, and large triangular-shaped ears proportionately too large for its head. It was very sleek, not stocky or muscular at all, and with long whiskers.

It was ambling slowly, but when it spotted us it stopped in its tracks, then disappeared into undergrowth. We moved closer to see if we could see it again, but didn't. We were convinced that the animal was a cat, but unlike any species we recognised, and it moved in a feline manner. We stood stunned for a while, me especially because back in 1986 my husband, two sons and myself had seen a large black panther on Exmoor and I couldn't believe that I have seen two large cats in my lifetime, although this latest one was not like the panther I saw then. I was very relieved to discover your website and read about all the other sightings – surely people take the existence of large cats roaming the countryside seriously now?'

Tout Quarry – 26 July 2004

Rod Wild, WPBC Borough Dog Warden, wrote: 'I enclose a copy of my diary entry for Monday 26 July 2004 which may be of interest. "Very quiet at work. Overcast but warm … . At Tout I saw a strange animal. It could have been a fox but was not quite right. It was about the same size as Mitch (19½ lb) but jet black with a fine coat and a brush which drooped rather like a fat lamb's. The face (I saw it from behind) didn't appear foxy. It was clearly moving steadily and unhurriedly and not jerkily like a fox. I resisted the temptation to give chase but took my time to come round that way (it was not the way back for us). Torn (Rod's dog) who is fox mad did not give any indication of scent … . I rang the local fox man who knows a lot on the island and he also was of the opinion that it was not a fox or domestic/feral cat. In his nocturnal wanderings he has seen similar over the years and, given the time of year, thinks it could have been a young 'big cat' looking for territory, perhaps from Chesil Beach, and may not settle."

He added: 'About 10 years ago, parked in a lay-by at Arundel, I looked up to the top of a ride and saw a big cat the size of a Lab, jet black, long tail, sniffing round. I walked up to the spot, but it had gone. A friend of mine has also had a sighting in Portland at Verne Common, and was amazed.'

Southwell – 16 September 2006

A witness wrote: 'Just for your records I am 24 and work as an engineer on Portland. I live in Southwell on Portland, and last Saturday night I was in bed and around 11.30 p.m. I heard the foxes in the playing field at the back of my house fighting. This I am told is what the sort of screech/bark noise I hear at night is, but it kept on going for 5 minutes. So I got out of bed and looked out of the window to see if I could see the foxes, but to my amazement I saw a big black thing near the goal post. The noise from the foxes was still going on, but I think they must have been in the bushes near the business park entrance; anyway I kept watching this black animal, thinking it must be a dog, but it started to move away and it didn't look right as it walked. It looked weird and had a rounded, long body – so this made me even more interested. So I watched it stroll to the other side of the park where there is the end of another road, looking to see if I could see anyone around as it is popular during the day with dog walkers, but I could not see anyone. It walked down the middle of the road where I could see it better because of the street lights. This must be around a hundred metres away now, and it definitely did not look like a dog. The bottom third of the very long tail was curved upwards to the right. It didn't move when walking as dogs' tails usually do. I carried on watching it to see if I could see an owner but still nothing. It walked off in the middle of the road until the point where the road bends and it went out of my vision. I think it is about time one is caught to prove this one way or the other – do they really exist or are they only in people's minds? Where do they live during the day? Why have no bodies been found?'

🐾 Powerstock

Railway bridge, Nettlecombe – 2000 or 2001

Mr and Mrs Connaughton were walking along the lane between Marsh Farm and North Eggardon Farm near Nettlecombe and probably about 300 yards beyond the railway bridge, when, Mrs Connaughton wrote, they saw a dog-sized black cat: 'My husband saw it first, on a track at the side of the field on the left-hand side of the road, i.e. he saw the whole animal. I saw it about 30 yards into the field of wheat, and therefore I could see only along the top of its back and its feline tail. However, it was obvious what it was It was the size of a medium-sized Labrador and had apparently been resting in the crop of wheat. It seemed to get up and stretch. We stood and watched it for several minutes and then it appeared to lie down again. My husband then walked into the field towards it to try to get a better view, while I walked into the next field for the same reason because it was only a few yards from the dividing hedge, but to no avail. There was no further sighting of it. The wheat was well grown but not yet fully grown so the time of year must have been early summer. As for our reaction at the time, we were certainly not nervous, just fascinated to actually be watching this elusive creature that we had heard so much about! Other than the fact that it was definitely feline and black, we have no idea what it was.'

Powerstock Station and Beaminster tunnel – 2003

The witness said she had been aware of other sightings, because her neighbour, Mrs B, had encountered a big cat at Powerstock in 1998. On this occasion she was taking her dogs for a walk when she spotted a brown-coloured big cat in a field opposite Powerstock Station. 'It was bigger than my collies, with a long, thick tail. It just stood and looked at me – and I and my dogs looked at it. My lurcher-type, who chases anything, made no move towards it. Then it just went – disappeared into the hedge.' She and her dogs hurried off in the opposite direction.

In the same year, Mrs B's son had been sitting inside a field gate, near Beaminster tunnel, and a large black panther-like feline walked past him.

Abandoned railway near Nettlecombe – 23 April 2008

The witness wrote: 'I was just out on a run on the old railway line near Nettlecombe. I saw a big cat, slightly smaller than my medium-sized Labrador. It was bright orangey-red with pointy (lynx-like) ears and a very long tail.'

🐾 Purbeck, Isle of

6 August 2005

Naturalist Jonathan McGowan wrote: 'I was photographing spiders on heathland in Purbeck. I was walking through purple moor grass, that forms tussocks, when I became aware of a swishing noise of something walking ahead of me. I noticed the back of an animal just 25 ft away. It had a grey/brown russet tinge. I saw its shoulders rippling; its head was held low, walking under the tussocks. I noticed that it was a cat and there was a pungent musky smell in the air. I parted the grass and noticed that I was walking on a well-worn path, muddy with footprints of puma-like spoor. I lost sight of the animal but purposely returned the next night, though found no sign of anything but sika deer. But just before dawn I checked out a small group of hinds, and noticed an animal separated from the rest, lying down in the heather. I presumed it was a calf, it remained motionless for over 20 minutes. It was misty so I could not see any detail. Suddenly from a block of gorse about 20 yards from the animal, another animal raced towards it. The stationary animal leaped about 5 ft into the air vertically, as the other passed underneath. Then both animals dashed into the gorse from where the second animal had come. As the stationary animal jumped I could plainly see it was a cat. Everything about it was puma, but smallish, body length about 3 ft, with a long thick tail. They were cubs, frolicking. It all took 3 or 4 seconds of very fast activity. Then no more. There was no sound from the cats.'

🐾 Rampisham

Crewkerne road – 13 May 2006

Felicity Warner saw a huge black cat cross the Crewkerne road above Rampisham. She wrote: 'I have been thinking more about the black cat and I'm trying to find a picture of a similar one in your book. It was certainly jet black and quite tall; stocky but also elegant and powerful. Although it passed out of view quickly it wasn't darting rapidly but seemed to be focused and confident. The tail was elongated and looped up at the end. Those are just my impressions made in that snapshot of the moment.'

🐾 Salway Ash

Pineapple Lane – 1995

Within 2 days of sightings at Symondsbury, a woman reported to the police that she had seen a big cat-like animal along Pineapple Lane.

🐾 Shaftesbury

August 2002

A 4-ft-long black cat was apparently disturbed by farm machinery at the back of the witness's house. He described it as 'black and brown, with stuck-up ears' and a long tail.

🐾 Sherborne

Sherborne Castle – 2004

A witness wrote: 'About 2 years ago at 6 a.m. my wife and I saw what only can be described as a panther. The sighting was south of Sherborne in Dorset. We did not tell anyone else as we thought people would say we were a little strange. I originally saw the big cat from about 200 yards as I came round the bend by Sherborne Castle, next to the garden centre. I said to my wife, "Look at that!" I slowed my car to a stop and managed to stop less than 12 ft away from it. We were this close to the cat for over 30 seconds and had a clear unobstructed view of the animal. It did not have a collar and was most definitely a panther. The cat did not seem bothered at all and just kept looking around the edge of the hedging/fencing there. It then looked as us, and then went through the fence out of our sight. My wife is an animal expert and I know the difference through seeing cats abroad and in wildlife parks. We do not drink and do not take any illegal drugs.'

Sherborne Castle – Autumn 2007

Another witness reported: 'We were driving in the early hours by some grassland with railings adjacent to Castle Garden Centre, Sherborne, when what seemed to be a big cat-type cub passed right in front of our car and over some railings. It was very dark, large and solid, and cat-like – exactly like a black puma cub … . It also had the long, looped down then up tail.'

🐾 Shipton Gorge

1997/1998

The witness was driving along the A35 and had taken the turning to Shipton Gorge. At the bottom of the hill she saw a large feline animal cross the road in front of her, from one hedge to another. She was excited and rushed home to tell her husband. Unusually this big cat was black, 'but mottled'.

🐾 Sixpenny Handley

New Town – 4 March 2002
The *Dorset Echo* reported: 'A milk tanker driver claimed he saw a big black panther-type cat near the tiny hamlet of New Town between Blandford and Sixpenny Handley.'

September 2002
A woman out walking her dog near the Dorset border encountered 'an Alsatian-sized, black, panther-like cat'. It watched her from only 20 yards away before making off.

Bottlebrush Down – 8 May 2006
The following sighting took place at noon. The witness parked his car on a verge and saw 'two black things' in a field a quarter of a mile away. He looked through binoculars and saw what seemed to be big cat cubs, possibly about 5 months old, chasing leverets around the field. They were about 2.5 ft in length with long, thin tails. 'Very definitely cats', he said.

🐾 Stoke Abbott

Lewesdon Hill – historical account
The Lewesdon Hill area has been associated with mystery felines for many years it seems. Mr Wakely recalls that in his youth, 40 or so years ago, they used to trap rabbits on the hill at night using long nets. On three or four occasions, he remembers, they found a large wild cat also entangled in the nets. These animals seemed to be twice the size of a normal domestic cat, were dark tabby in colour and very fierce.

Lewesdon Hill

Lewesdon Hill – September 1994

A panther-like animal was seen by Frank Smith driving along the B3162 near Lewesdon Hill at 8.30 on a sunny morning. Mr Smith was near Buck's Head, and pulled off the road to watch the cat walking a line between fields of crops and grass. He described it as being 'black, about the size of an Alsatian dog, and resembling a panther, with a small head and small upright ears. It had a deep chest and a long tail which appeared to be tufted at the end. It loped along like a cat.'

Lewesdon Hill – 29 August and October 2003

The *Bridport and Lyme Regis News* reported a sighting of a wolf: 'Pensioner Dudley Tolley, near Stoke Abbott, says he isn't crying wolf – he really did see one on Sunday! Mr Dudley Tolley of Stoke Knapp Farm, who has lived in the area all his life, said he was out checking his cattle in the early morning, about 6.15 a.m. He was going along the lane opposite the house, and saw it coming down the lane from Lewesdon Hill towards him. He saw it before it saw him. He said: "When it was 15 yards away from me I could see it was a wolf. It was dark grey, taller than a large Alsatian, with spindly legs – not as thick-set as an Alsatian. It looked at me as though it was thinking shall I go back or shall I go through the hedge? It was unhurried. Then it went through the hedge, and I went to the gate to see where it had gone but there was no sign of it. It was a beautiful animal in very good condition. I have never seen a wolf in the wild before." Mr Tolley said he contacted the police who did not seem interested and also DEFRA's animal health team. "I am hoping someone will arrange to capture it", he said. In October 2003 he saw it again from a hundred yards away, chasing sheep. "It went after them so slowly. Not darting about fast like a dog does. I have shot an Alsatian doing it, so I know the difference. When it saw me it went off fast."'

Knapp Farm – 3 April 2006

Richard Warner reported: 'I was so excited to see a large black cat, with white, furry, seemingly boot-clad or almost, feet, at Knapp Farm, Stoke Abbott on Monday 3rd April … . It's odd because the area around Knapp Farm is a rather eerie spot; then to see the cat almost made me jump out of my skin.'

🐾 Stourhead (Wiltshire)

March 2004 and 14 June 2005

Jacqueline Cooke had gone to the bathroom window and in the light of dawn had seen a black big cat walking along the garden wall. The bathroom is on a level with the window as the garden slopes towards it, and the animal was about 30 ft away. Her son Sam had pooh-poohed her sighting, as, he said himself, he is very sceptical about anything that might be called out of the ordinary. However, 15 months later he had an experience that made him change his mind: 'It was 8.30 last night, 14 June 2005', Sam recounted, 'and I went outside to call my dog, but she didn't come. She was sitting on the edge of the lawn which overlooks a steep bank which descends to a rushy bottom with the forest beyond. She was looking towards the forest and seemed on edge. I looked down the bank and saw bounding along the bottom what I at first thought was one of our neighbour's black Labradors – but then realised this was a slightly bigger animal with a much, much longer tail. It was about 25 m away and running straight into the forest. It moved in a cat-like way – more elegant than a dog – but it was obviously not a domestic cat. I was amazed. My dog was just sitting there looking at it as if amazed too. I rang my father to tell him.' (See photo in Introduction.)

The view from Jacqueline Cooke's bathroom window, from where she watched a black ABC walking along the top of the garden wall

🐾 Stourpaine

Between Compton Abbas and Stourpaine – Summer 1994

Fiona Huston wrote: 'Sorry this is an old sighting, but it still amazes me to this day … . I had been working in Bristol on a Friday night in the summer of 1994 and drove down to Swanage across country, leaving Bristol around 11.30 p.m. in order to spend the weekend with friends on the beach. I remember having all the windows down in my VW Golf, driving through Roman-named villages, along almost single-track roads in some places. I was on the A350 between Compton Abbas and Stourpaine, and had to slow right down to do a sharp left bend in the road. Once I'd turned, there staring at me were two reflective yellow-green eyes about 3 ft off the ground. It was a large black cat sitting in the road. I stopped no more than 10 ft away from where it was sitting. I'm afraid that when I stopped, because the windows were open and it was about 1 or 2 in the morning, I suddenly realised I was in the middle of nowhere with a creature sat in front of me that I had not expected, so all I could think about was getting the windows up and locking the doors. It wasn't afraid at all. Once I'd put up the windows it walked towards the car slightly and then across the beam of the lights and down the passenger side. Its back was about the height of the front of the car (about 30 inches high) and tip of nose to tip of tail was almost as long as the width of the car (about 5 ft wide). The tail was long and thin and held off the ground, curling up at the end. It loped and had a large head. It wasn't in a rush at all. My instant and only name I could give it was a panther. The whole episode probably only lasted 1 minute or so. As soon as it was clear of my wheels I put my foot down and then had a panic attack! When I told my friends they laughed and said it must have been a badger. This put me off making a fuss about it at the time, but I know what I saw.'

✖ Studland

Blue Lagoon, Sandbanks – June 2001

Sid Shaw reported the following experience: 'My wife is a metal detectorist, so we often get up at dawn. We were driving on the Sandbanks road parallel with the harbour at about 4.30 a.m., but it was June and so was already light. We were near the Blue Lagoon when we saw a big cat – bigger than an Alsatian, mastiff-sized – going into a garden. We were about 15 yards from it, but saw only the back half of it as it disappeared around a gatepost. It looked like the back end of a puma, but black. What was most unusual was the long tail, drooping down level with the ground and with that peculiar turn at the end where the last 9 inches or so loop upwards again. We both looked at it, and each other. We didn't speak for a while, and then we said to each other, "What the hell was that?" We didn't stop because we thought "Nah! – it couldn't be." I'm 76 and I've seen cats in the wild. In fact I've been face to face with a tiger in Malaya while scouting in the jungle during the war. We both retreated from each other as fast as possible, but I wasn't too afraid as I had a gun. We're used to seeing foxes at that time in the morning, but this wasn't a normal animal. We didn't know what the devil it was. It made us think. We didn't report it because people think you're nutty if you report a thing like that! But it does shake you up a bit, doesn't it?'

14 April 2006

Jonathan McGowan reported: 'I was at Studland at dusk. The Canada geese started honking, and the herd of sika deer looked toward the edge of the plain. The small herd of horses whinnied and galloped away. Magpies and crows gave alarm calls. After 5 minutes of not seeing anything, a black, lithe figure trotted along the hedgerow, sniffed, then rubbed its chin on a fencepost. It walked about 60 or 70 ft along the path, then quickly doubled back and disappeared behind gorse bushes. I could clearly see it through my binoculars. I was about 600 yards away, and although it was almost dark, my binoculars are good in dull light. The animal had a thick neck, big head, surely a male. Its body was about 4 ft long, with a long but not extremely thin tail.'

✖ Sturminster Newton

Earliest records

The earliest record of a big cat in Dorset comes from a 1907 manuscript entitled *Reminiscences of Sturminster Newton*, by Robin Young, and quoted in *Dark Dorset Tales of Mystery, Wonder and Terror* by R.J. Newland and M.J. North. Young was a Sturminster man, looking back to his schooldays in the 1820s. He remarked that teachers should 'not allow absurd stories to be told before timid and sensitive children'. For example:

'A story was often told them of a wild and savage cat which haunted the remains of the old castle and was often seen on Newton Hill. Such horrid tales were told of this monster cat, with eyes as big as tea saucers that many children were afraid to pass that way, and not only children but grown-up people would be so afraid that they would walk on the main road below the hill to avoid the creature. I am pleased to know that foolish tale is quite forgotten'. According to Jeremy Harte (*Cuckoo Pounds and Singing Barrows,* 1986): 'In a more recent source, the legend is of a terrifying creature which ran along a track parallel to the main road at a place called The Hollow … near the old castle at Newton. A local clergyman knew someone who spoke of it as a dog in 1965.'

Bagber – 29 August 2000

The *Western Daily Press* reported: 'Farmer's son Chris Griffin, of Fifehead Neville, believes the animal he saw in a field near Bagber, Sturminster Newton in Dorset, must have been a big cat. He and four other 19-year-old friends were out rabbiting in a field above Cutt Mill at around 9.30 one night 2 weeks ago when they saw the beast in their headlights. Recalling his sighting yesterday Chris said: "It was four times the size of a normal cat, and black. It was 150 yards away and going at a fast pace, but I could see straight away it wasn't a dog, from its shape. We held it in the spotlight for about 3 minutes until it disappeared. Fifteen months ago we lost four sheep which had their throats ripped out. When dogs kill sheep you can usually see marks on their backs where they have been dragged down – and smaller dogs go for the legs. But these sheep had all just had their throats ripped out. There have been other sightings of an animal around Bagber. I know it is difficult to prove, but we know what we saw."'

Stour Valley Path, Hinton St Mary – 29 May 2004

Chris and Derek Ormesher were walking the Stour Valley path at about 11.30 one sunny morning, and were a few miles south of, and walking towards, Marnhull. Chris wrote: 'We both saw a large ginger animal walking away from the pond that we were passing, about 50 yards away. The animal had a long tail which was noticeably ringed with darker fur at the end, and had large pointed ears and markings on its legs. The tail behaved more like a lion's tail rather than a domestic cat's tail because it pointed downwards and then along the floor and swished as the animal walked. At first we were scared stiff because we initially thought it was bigger than it actually was. When we saw the tail, its shape and how it was moving, we thought it was a lion (which obviously it wasn't). It seemed to be about the size of a springer spaniel. It was walking slowly away from the pond, in broad daylight. It didn't seem worried when it spotted us. It turned its head to have a good look at us and then disappeared into a hedge. From looking at pictures on the internet it was definitely a jungle cat.'

Hinton St Mary – 11 November 2007

The witness was driving on the road near Hinton St Mary between Marnhull and Sturminster Newton. 'I was driving towards Sturminster and the animal ran across the road and jumped through the hedgerow just in front of my head lights. I hit the brakes but didn't get a clear sighting – just saw a long tail and long body and it moved in a cat-like way. My daughter (18) is also certain she saw a big black cat in a field about

6 weeks ago on the same stretch of road – we turned the car round but it was gone when we went back. Very long tail which was the main thing I noticed.'

🐾 Swanage

Ulwell – 1906

The folklorist Jeremy Harte recorded: 'On the Island of Purbeck the old road used to pass through a toll gate just outside Ulwell, and a cottage beside the road was home to the witch, Jinny Gould. She used to sit out on the gate at nights in the form of a cat, getting a lot of fun out of terrifying travellers, until one drunken carter picked up enough daring to land her a blow across the back with his whip. Suddenly the cat vanished, and back in the cottage Jinny lay dead (Luckham 1906). Today both the toll gate and the cottage are gone, although haunted gates survive elsewhere in the county. Normally it is ghosts which sit on these liminal markers, not witches, although a cat-witch is reported from a farm gate in Cheshire (Briggs 1970: B2.628). A Dorset witch is much more likely to take the form of a hare. One of these animals used to linger around the hills near Ulwell, teasing hunters by running in and out of range, but never getting hurt. Nobody had the cunning to load their gun with a silver sixpence, which is what men ought to carry when they suspect they are dealing with a quarry which is not right.' (*At the Edge*, No.6, 1997)

🐾 Symondsbury

6 February 1995

A farmer, John Turner, of Highway Farm, saw a large 'lynx-like' animal while driving to work at 7.20 one morning. He watched it as it ambled across the road in front of his van. It was 'about the size of a Boxer dog, very compact, with a short tail and biggish feet. It was very furry, with mottled light brown, dark brown and almost black spots. It also had very pointed ears'. He reported it to the police.

Colmer's Hill – 23 May 1995

A 'large feline animal' was seen at Colmer's Hill.

Miles Cross – 10 August 1998

Stuart wrote: 'It was spring and the event took place near Miles Cross on the outskirts of Bridport between 8 and 8.30 a.m. The day was clear, although the sun was still very low in the sky and giving long shadows. I was driving to work and took West Road to the bypass, turning right towards Chideock. As I turned onto the bypass I looked into my rear-view mirror and saw a large cat followed by three smaller cats crossing the main road at speed, away from Bridport. The larger cat was about the size of a fox, with the smaller ones the size of domestic cats. There is no doubt in my mind that these were not foxes, nor were they dogs. The body shapes and movements were definitely feline although far smaller than what I would call a panther. Each of the cats seemed jet black, but with the sun behind it was difficult to judge their colour.'

Ryeberry Hill – 29 September 1998

The *Dorset Echo* reported: 'Postman Joe Tait had his dogs with him, a Jack Russell and a collie cross, when he climbed over the fence behind his home in West Road at 3.10 p.m. on Saturday to walk around Ryeberry Hill. As he entered the field he was amazed to see, just 60 yards away, a large cat-like creature astride the body of a sheep, tearing its heart out. The creature caught sight of Mr Tait and ran off with his dogs in hot pursuit – but it outran them easily and vanished into a spinney at the back of Ryeberry Hill. At least half a dozen sheep have been found ripped apart in the area over the past week or so. Local farmers say they will now set up armed evening patrols in a bid to hunt down whatever is killing their valuable stock. Mr Tait said: "I actually thought at first it was a badger eating the sheep. It was holding the carcase down with its feet and ripping it up. The creature was a bit smaller than a collie dog and it was all black with a long tail. … I wouldn't have believed it, but I am 100% certain of what I saw – it was no more than 60 yards away."'

Westerly Hill – 25 August 2002

It was exactly 5 a.m. when Mr Davis and his wife were awakened by a spine-chilling noise: 'It was like a screech owl, dog, cat all put together. The following early morning – the curious thing was it was at exactly 5 a.m. again – we heard it again and got up and looked outside.' From the window they saw a large black cat, 4–6 ft in length and with a long tail. Mr Davis told me: 'It sat still on a low wall in our garden for about 10 minutes, but when we opened the window it

The wall outside Mr and Mrs Davis' bedroom, on which a black panther-like cat yowled on two consecutive nights

bounded off. I was mostly struck by the teeth. They were white and showing clearly.' Mr Davis had given much thought to the sighting since it happened. He showed me a 3-ft green wire fence next to the low wall in question, which they had just put up at the time to keep in their new puppy. He wondered if the cat was yowling because it had found its route impeded. He also began to ask around for news of other sightings, and found several people who had had encounters with mystery animals. A friend had found a deer killed and gutted on his tennis court; a rider had seen a big cat on the old railway line; someone from Lyme Regis told him: 'We see it every day drinking from our bowser'. And several times he came across a rumour that '7 or 8 years ago someone saw one dragging a deer under a gate at Highlands End Caravan Park'. That rumour included the idea that this had been hushed up as being bad for tourism.

❧ Tarrant Rushton

24 June 2005

The witness recounted: 'At 8.45 this evening my wife and I were driving along the road from Tarrant Rushton old airfield towards Witchampton. At one point a large, all-black cat bounded from the left hedge across the road in just two long swift leaps and through the opposite hedge. We must have been 100 ft away, but both of us saw it clearly. It was of muscular build and clearly agile ... We stopped the car and standing on a bank could see something black (now probably about 125 yards away) searching between standing crops and the hedge. Two horses in a nearby field had seen it and with their ears up were looking across to the same spot.'

❧ Turnworth

29 October 2006

Mark Benwell wrote: 'I have seen today a large black cat, possibly a panther, on the road outside the village of Turnworth near Blandford at 7.55 a.m. It was chasing a small deer across the road in front of me. They both darted through a hole in the hedge and ran across the field. The cat was huge and had a very long tail, but I could not see the head well as it was moving fast. I thought these things were not real until today.' He added: 'I was driving to a metal detecting club outing and I was alone. I was listening to the GPS telling me how far I had to go when they ran out about 10 yards in front of me across the grass verge from right to left through the hedge. I stopped the car and stood on the seal of my car door to see over the hedge, and watched them move fast away. It was about 500 yards away from the church, on a very small road where just about two cars can pass. I did not even tell the others as they would think I was mad; it was only when I got home and told the wife she said I should report it. I hope this helps some. I won't forget it, I know that.'

🐾 Wareham

Early 1990s

There were apparently multiple sightings on Forestry Commission land around Wareham, but unfortunately details are not available. If anyone can throw light on this period I would like to hear from them.

Arne road – 5 April 2004

Mrs Joan Hatch and her daughter Anne and son Robert were driving very slowly along the road from Wareham to Arne, hoping to glimpse and photograph deer, as they often do, when a large cat-like creature slid down from a bank to the right of the road and crossed no more than about 3 m in front of them. Mrs Hatch recalled: 'It was glossy black and about the size of a Labrador but longer. It looked rounded and well fed. The way it ran was peculiar – racing across at high speed in a crouching position, as if on its stomach. I can't say I saw a tail, but we were so taken by surprise.' Robert was in the back seat with the camera, looking the other way, but alerted by Joan and Anne he saw it as it reached the left-hand side of the road, and ran up and along a parallel ridge for a few seconds, before disappearing into woods. 'It was a shiny black animal – it had a sheen. It looked rounded, not sinewy. The speed it moved was incredible. We waited, watching to see where it went, but it had gone.' The Hatches are experienced spotters of wildlife 'but this was quite new'. Mrs Hatch added that they had heard about sightings of big cats but 'until you see it for yourself you never quite take it in'.

Arne road – 9 May 2004

The Hatch family (see above) again saw not one but two big cats at 8.15 p.m. on the Arne road, very near the first sighting they had had. The cats had appeared racing, cheetah-like, along a firebreak that runs parallel to the road, visible through the thin

The Hatch family searching for paw prints after spotting two black panther-like animals racing along this forest path near Arne

brush that separates the firebreak from the road. This time they noticed long tails flowing out behind them. At a huge pile of wood chippings they lost sight of the animals, and their subsequent search failed to produce any further glimpses. Anne had spotted them first and afterwards she felt quite trembly, 'almost as if she had seen a phantom'.

Wareham Forest – 5 October 2004

At 10.30 a.m. Mr Batchelor was walking his lurcher in Wareham Forest. He had deliberately chosen a quiet part of the forest as his dog was in season. It was a quiet, clear and bright day. Suddenly he saw that his dog had seen something as she was looking fixedly ahead and her hackles had risen and she was making quiet barks. Mr Batchelor said: 'She spots deer before I do, so I looked to see what it was. About 200 yards ahead, crossing the track, was a black, Labrador-sized, cat-like animal … . What catches your eye is the gait of the animal – it was just strolling. I don't think it was aware we were there. It had the typical, very long, curved tail – the classic thing – and its style of walking was definitive. I might have thought it was my imagination if it hadn't been for the dog seeing it first. It certainly stirred her up – and dogs haven't got any axe to grind have they?' He was not afraid and hurried to the spot where the big cat had been, but there was no further sign of it. He looked for paw prints, but the ground was too dry.

26 October 2004

Mrs A of Weymouth wrote: 'My daughter and I were driving through wooded country near Wareham, along a track which has undergrowth and trees on either side. Suddenly a huge black animal came out of the undergrowth a few yards in front of the car and leapt right from one side of the track to the other. We had a clear, close view of it. It was completely black and had large paws and a head like that of a domestic cat. It was bigger than a Labrador (we used to have one) – about 5.5 ft long – and was quite slender. I think it saw and heard the car and that is why it leapt to the other side instead of walking. It obviously had its route clear in its mind and it wanted to enter the woods which were on the other side of the road. My daughter and I were completely shocked and looked at each other in amazement. I then stopped the car because I was hoping to get a better look. We both got out and looked into the ferns on our right. Unfortunately we did not see the creature again and as we travelled back to Weymouth we agreed that getting out of the car had not been a wise thing to do considering the size of the creature. We were shocked because the animal was not what you expect to see in the British countryside – it was a bit alarming.'

East Holme to Wool road – 16 December 2004

John Kitching wrote: 'I was driving on the East Holme to Wool road near Wareham, just opposite the army firing range, at about 6.30 in the evening. I saw what I thought was a deer in the hedge ahead in the headlights and slowed right down because they often run across at the last minute, so I was going about 10 mph when I passed … . And it was a deer, but a dead deer with something about the same size crouched upon it. I was sure it was a big cat. I was quite shaken – hairs standing up at the back of the neck, etc. I drove home and told everybody. But I didn't know there had been any other sightings so I convinced myself (and was convinced by others!) I must have imagined it. It could have been another deer looking at a dead deer. But we have cats and the way it was crouching, it was just like an animal with its prey.

Possibly unrelated, but about the same time last year a week or so after the first sighting, in fields near Wool, about 2 miles from that sighting, my dog started barking very strangely and when I got to him we were both staring at a freshly killed deer which had been disembowelled by something very big or someone with a very sharp knife. There was no sign of anybody or anything close by. The dog seemed more alarmed than I would have expected for him seeing a dead deer. Since then I've looked for signs but haven't seen any.'

Carey, Wareham Forest – 11 November 2005

A witness wrote: 'I'm writing to report a sighting of what I believe to have been a black panther, at Carey, near Wareham, just inside Wareham Forest, late on the night of 11 November 2005. I was sitting reading at home, when my 16-month-old German shepherd heard a noise at about 11.30 p.m. and then became very on edge. I thought he might have heard people coming back from the pub or maybe a local fox or stag, but after 10 minutes of unsettled behaviour I decided to let him outside into the back garden, which is enclosed by a 6-ft fence all round. He went out, stood there, sniffed a bit and then turned on his tail and came back inside very quickly. I didn't think any more of this until about midnight when I let him outside before I went to bed. As I always do, I made him sit by the inner porch door and wait while I opened the outer door and "checked" that it was ok for him to go outside. The moment I opened the front door, I immediately saw this large black shadow on the driveway. It was late and I was tired, so for a split second my rational mind registered this as a large black cat sitting or resting on the driveway with a huge black shadow making it look bigger. But as I opened the door I saw it begin to get up and I realised that there was no shadow and this was no ordinary cat.

Whatever our nationality or culture, we all have an instinctive knowing of "danger", and at that point all my courage left me and instinctively I immediately called my poor young dog, who rushed to the door, took one look at the creature and began to leap towards it. The big cat immediately responded by turning and taking one huge leap into the copse a few feet behind it, on the other side of the driveway. It was then that I saw just how big it was. It was much too big for a domestic cat; it was the size of a working Labrador, but with the litheness, confidence and thickness of leg of a panther. My dog chased the cat into the copse and I heard him growl a very cautious warning growl (at least, I assumed at the time that it was him), quite unlike anything I have heard him make before. At that point, my dog came rushing back inside. Tonight, he has been very cautious about going outside again and steers clear of the area where the "panther" was sitting and, I have to admit, I've been very cautious before opening the front door! I checked for footprints in the copse and found only large prints which I took to be my dog's. The ground there is covered in soft earth and leaves at the moment which makes identification difficult.'

Trigon Estate – 31 January 2006

Paul Webber was out walking his dog at 7.30 a.m., but at this stage was in his car. He saw a sandy-coloured cat, spaniel-sized, standing about 30 ft from his car. It then went 'skipping up the lane' and out of sight.

East Holme – December 2007

A university lecturer in criminology was driving on the road that runs past East Holme Rifle Range at 8.20 p.m. when she saw what she described as a panther just the Wool side of the ford. She said: 'I came round a corner and saw these eyes on the roadside verge – there are usually deer on this road so I slowed down – but these were different, whitey blue. I thought "What's that?" and started to slow in case it jumped out – then saw this large animal on the verge of the road. It was very close – about 6 ft away, and I couldn't believe what I was seeing – I was stunned – pinching myself! It was large Labrador dog height, but much longer, 4–5 ft long without the tail; very sturdy and muscular, fit looking. It was looking at me, or into the lights; its face was big and very contoured, a very hard-looking face. I must have stared at it for half a minute before I pulled myself together and really started to examine it. I could see the whiskers, and it had what looked like a squirrel dangling from its mouth. I seemed to be mesmerised … and we looked at each other for about a minute or so, and then I had the irrational idea of locking the car door. As I moved, it backed off slowly – still staring into the lights – and into the woods behind it.'

Carey to Trigon Estate – 7 April 2008

Brian Mabbutt wrote: 'I was driving on a back road between Carey, Wareham, and the private Trigon Estate yesterday at approximately 3 p.m. when a large cat walked across the road in front of me. It was possibly about 2 ft 6 inches in height, with a long, slender, strong body, and a long tail nearly down to the ground and just curling away behind. It was dark in colour – maybe darkish brown, grey or black. Unfortunately it was about 50 m in front of me and crossed the road so quickly that I was too stunned to take it in completely. It had a smallish head and must have had small ears because they were not prominently sticking up to see. It did not look towards me, just went from one side of the road, having emerged from undergrowth, to the other side, disappearing again into undergrowth. The weather was really good yesterday; bright sunshine with a little cloud, and visibility during the afternoon was really good. It was so clear; I could not mistake what I'd seen!'

🐾 West Bay

Cliff path – August 2005

A witness wrote: 'On this particular night I couldn't sleep, so as it was a particularly brilliant night for stars here in West Bay, I thought I'd walk up the cliff path a bit to get away from the light pollution and do a bit of stargazing. Found a nice bench, laid down – perfect, pitch black, loads of stars. Very relaxing, until a few minutes later, something large and dog-sized galloped at speed right up to the bench! I sat up with a start and the animal then shot off in another direction. It was then that I remembered my father's stories of seeing the 'beast of Dorset' several times and then I realised that maybe sitting alone in the pitch black in the Dorset countryside for the sake of astronomy wasn't one of my better ideas. I did not see the animal again unfortunately.'

🐾 Weymouth

Nothe Gardens – January/February 1981

A correspondent, Garry, reported: 'My sighting of a big black cat was round about January or February 1981. It was late morning and I was taking my sister's dog, a collie called Brandy, for a walk up the Nothe Gardens in Weymouth. On the way I decided to take Brandy up this rough alleyway for a change – down by the old Devenish brewery at the back of Newberry Road, a residential area but close enough to fields and trees, etc. When I got about 20 yards up the alleyway I couldn't believe my eyes what I was seeing ahead of me. I thought, "That's a big bloody cat!" It was pure black. I thought, "I'm not turning round and going back for no cat", and as I got closer and saw its big green eyes I felt the hairs go up on the back of my neck. Brandy the dog was as quiet as a mouse. I got to about 15 ft of it, and then decided I didn't have much else of an alternative but to turn round and go back the way I had come from. The cat was about 6 ft long, maybe 2.5–3 ft high, green eyes and long ropey tail. I've only told a handful of people about it in the last 24 years or so. At the time I was 25.'

Chafey's roundabout, Weymouth Way – 5 December 1995

The *Dorset Echo* reported: 'Portland van driver Chris Allen claims to have spotted a big cat-like creature near the Chafey's roundabout on Weymouth Way. He said: "As I approached, this big black animal suddenly appeared in front of me and crossed the road heading into the Radipole Nature Reserve. As it went it seemed to prowl like a wild cat and, judging by its size, there is no way it could have been a domestic moggy."'

The Swannery – 27 October 1998

Around this time the press was reporting sightings of the 'Beast of Westham'. An article in the *Dorset Echo* read: 'Helen Johnson and her partner were travelling home in a taxi close to the swannery in Westham, at about 2 a.m. "As we approached the roundabout close to Westham Bridge," she said, "we suddenly spotted this huge black cat-like creature running along the side of the road. It was definitely too big to be a domestic cat and it looked like a panther to me."'

The Swannery – December 2001

Emma wrote: 'It was in Weymouth, and it must have been early December in 2001. I used to drop my partner off to his fishing boat nearly every morning at about 4 o'clock, but this time I left a little earlier to go to the garage first, and so went a different route. On this morning I was driving to the local garage by the Swannery, via the roundabout off the bridge adjoining Abbotsbury Road. I couldn't believe what I then saw (and have stayed sceptical until I read your web page – wow, it really is true). I saw a big black cat of panther stance and size walking across the roundabout without a care in the world! It had a long stride. I have seen these in the zoo and would definitely say it was a panther.'

Weymouth to Bridport road – January 2002

In January 2002 Ray Toddington was driving on the coast road between Weymouth and Bridport when he saw what he described as a big cat run across the road. He said it was too big to be a domestic cat and had black markings on its nose and paws.

Benville Road and Chickerell Road – 10 May 2005

The local press reported: 'Eighty-year-old Joyce Ash of Tollerdown Road said she saw a big cat from her kitchen window on an empty garage forecourt at the top of Benville Road and Chickerell Road. She said: "I thought it was a fox at first. I watched it for about 10 minutes. It was the size of a big dog and it went off down Tollerdown Road. It was certainly a big cat and seemed to have a long tail with a big tuft on the end. It was very ugly looking."'

May 2005

The local press reported: 'William Willoughby spotted from his living-room window what he believes was a lynx, only yards from a playground in Weymouth. He said: "I came downstairs for a cigarette and opened the window. As I looked out – we have good street lighting here – I saw what I first thought was a fox. It was obviously a lynx, three times the size of any normal cat. It snarled up at me three times and I thought it was going to attack so I pulled up the window a bit. It stayed there for a good 4 or 5 minutes; I think it may have been cleaning itself. Then it jumped onto the back wall which is a good 6 ft high, and then into the back garden." Mr Willoughby described it as a lovely looking animal. It had mouse-coloured hair and big eyes like a domestic cat. After the animal had left, three domestic cats came and began sniffing at the spot where it had been stood. As fate would have it Mr Willoughby had turned off the CCTV only days before!'

Station Road bridge – Summer 2005

Phil Coombs wrote: 'I live on a farm in the Bincombe area. On my way home from working late in Weymouth one evening in the summer of 2005, as I passed under the bridge at Station Road I did my usual trick of amusing myself by finding the pitch of voice to which the bridge above resonates. I walked a little way and then was surprised by the sound of a grumpy cat. What startled me was that it was a lot louder and lower than your usual feline. I looked up into the bank of shrubs behind me and caught the reflection of a large pair of eyes, wide set, and a large dark cat-shaped head, just before it slipped away up a commonly used animal track and presumably off back to its secret place. I am a regular day and night walker, wildlife watcher and listener, and am quite accustomed to the sounds of the undergrowth, badgers grunting and growling, foxes' screams and the occasional pops and low brays of our beautiful Dorset deer. I have never heard any wild animals make the kind of sound this critter did. Although my glimpse of it was quick, the animal was, judging by the height of its head above the bank plants, about the size of a medium dog.'

Radipole Lake – 19 February 2006

Mr M. Franks and Ms A. Pitman were walking home from an evening in town at around 2.30 a.m. They wrote: 'We were walking along Radipole Park Drive which is next to the main part of Radipole Lake. There were few cars on the road, but as one of the cars approached we both thought we saw something standing half on the pavement about 20 ft in front of us, with its back end still submerged in the hedge. As we approached (cautiously) it stared at us for about 15 seconds, and when we were about 15 ft away it turned on its tail and headed back into the bushes along the side of the lake. With the light from the car and the various lamp posts we are sure it was roughly 2 m in length from nose to tail and stood about the height of an Alsatian dog, though it was far more muscular and had extremely sleek fur/hair. There is no doubt in our minds that this was not a dog, and was far too big to be a domestic cat.'

Littlemoor, Broadwey – 30 January 2007

Shirley Farrar was walking in the woods at Littlemoor at about 2.30 p.m. when she encountered a 'pure black big cat' only 30 ft away, and watched it for 20 seconds. She said: 'It was as big as my Doberman, I would say roughly 3 ft tall, including the tail about 5 or 6 ft long. The tail was long and carried low. I was walking my two dogs through woods when they flushed it out and gave chase. The dogs were going crazy and were very unsettled and edgy when they came back. I have also over the last 4 weeks found three deer carcasses completely stripped of all flesh; the last kill was only a day after the sighting.'

🐾 Wimborne Minster

Caravan site – May and September 2001

Alan Davis reported two sightings of a big cat at a caravan site near Wimborne in 2001. He wrote: 'The first sighting was in early May of that year just as the sun was going down. When I first saw it it was lying down and I thought it was a deer. I went over to some other people who were near to me and together we walked over to another caravan that was nearer to it. They said that they had seen it several times before. It got up and walked around the site, keeping to the hedgerow towards the Reception area. It was a large cat resembling a puma. I knew there was a lady who had a small dog in the area it was heading for, so I went the other way round to tell her to keep the dog inside. I then went over to Reception to see if it had come out there, but I had lost it. I had been at the site on a seasonal pitch since 1989 and this was the first year I had seen anything like this.

In September the same year I was again staying on the caravan site when, at about 6 pm., I saw it for the second time. It just sat there and looked at me as if posing for me, and didn't seem agitated by me walking towards it. As it is a large caravan site it must have got used to humans being around. I walked towards it and got to within 50 yards of it. It then stood up, walked towards the bushes, turned around and looked at me one more time and strolled off into the bushes. Next door is a site where Portacabins were stored. I gave it a few minutes and then went over to see where it had gone. There was a large hole dug under the fence into the site next door. The cat was about 4 ft in length and stood about 2 ft to 2 ft 6 inches high. Its tail was quite long and it curled up at the end when walking off. It was a sandy colour with almost white underside and its tail had dark rings around it. This

Close up of photo of a puma-like animal at a caravan park near Wimborne. (Photo credit: Alan Davis)

time I took several photos of it. At the time I took the photos the rabbits that had been running around had disappeared which was unusual as they used to stay out until it got dark.

I was reading the account on your website of the chap that saw a big cat on the A31. The place where he saw it was just the other side of the storage site where the cat I saw disappeared into.' (See Alan Blair's sighting below – 14 September 2004. Note, however, that his sighting was of a black big cat, rather than what sounds like the typical puma colouration of this one.)

October 2002

A witness spotted what she described as a 'definitely puma-like' animal; however, unlike a puma it was black. The following March, and very close to the previous sighting, two witnesses spotted what they first assumed was a deer, and which they then realised was a very large cat-like animal.

Wimborne bypass, near Esso garage – 14 September 2004

Alan Blair wrote: 'Just thought I would let you know that as a distinct non-believer in big cats I have just had a close encounter with one this morning. Going to work along the A31 Wimborne bypass on the Dorchester side of the Corfe Mullen Esso garage, a large Labrador-size black cat shot across the road 20–30 ft in front of me from right to left, disappearing into the hedgerow. It was about 7.20 a.m. and traffic was light at that time of the morning though there was an approaching lorry. Very graceful animal – most striking thing about it was both its "fluid" movement and this great long tail – I would say that it was the same length as its body, U-shaped as well. Didn't stop as it was chucking down heavily, but I was completely awestruck I think. Stunned. Pretty amazing thing to see on a Dorset road. Hmm, this is going to do my credibility good at work!'

Pamphill – March 2005

Karen Thomson reported: 'It was about 8 weeks ago. My father and mother were travelling in their car towards Blandford on the Wimborne to Badbury Rings road. My mother believes she saw the animal in a field somewhere after the turning to Pamphill, Wimborne, but before the turning to Kingston Lacy House, on the left-hand side of the road (travelling towards Blandford). She originally thought it was a very large black dog, but she felt that the tail was far too long and hung differently and the head was too small, more cat-like.'

Pamphill – 30 April 2005

James Moran wrote: 'As we were setting out to walk along the river at Pamphill (near the footbridge if you know the area) my family and I noticed a black object in a nearby field as we were looking at a hare. As it appeared to be still and black we didn't know what it was. It then started walking across the field. It then became obvious it was a large black cat, larger than an adult Labrador. It wandered across the field towards some sheep, but then made its way up the field and went through a hedgerow. It looked like a small black panther with shortish legs and long tail. It walked very deliberately and sleekly yet quite quickly. The sheep, hare and rabbits in the field didn't seem to notice or care about the animal and the 'panther' didn't seem interested in them, which was odd. I tried to get a picture of it, but by the time the camera was got out of its case and switched on I only managed to get a bad photograph of its behind. We are certain it wasn't any normal wild or domestic animal and was some kind of large cat.'

Giddy Lake – 3 October 2005

Mrs Susan Hughes reported: 'At approximately 9.30 am on Monday whilst driving down Giddy Lake in Wimborne I was looking from my right to my left, admiring the properties, and spotted in an overgrown area of woodland a Labrador-sized black cat with an angular-shaped head, sitting on its haunches … . I stopped the car and backed up to see the creature again for a few seconds, before it seemed to lift into the air in a pouncing movement and disappeared into the brambles and bushes. My brother who was with me in the car is not as convinced as I am as to what I saw, but he did not have as clear a view as me. I am not from this area and knew nothing of the so-called Dorset big cats.'

18 November and 30 December 2005

Alice Lee has twice spotted a lynx-like cat near Wimborne. She wrote: 'I have seen it on one stretch of back lane near Wimborne – there is a mixture of woodland, fields and heathland there. Both times I have just seen its back end disappear through a hedge off the road. It is a sandy-coloured cat, approximately the size of a large Labrador with very strong-looking back legs. I saw only the rump both times, and noticed that it had a stump for a tail. I would say it was a lynx.

The first time I was sure of what I had seen, but my partner mocked me so I then wondered if I had really seen a lynx. The second time we both saw it and my partner had to agree with me that it was a big cat.'

March 2006 onwards

The witness wrote that he and his family have had several sightings over 18 months, 'usually at dusk or early evening but, on at least one occasion, in broad daylight in the afternoon'. He described the cat as jet black, with no visible markings. 'It has short ears, a low-slung body and a long, drooping tail curling slightly up towards the end. I would estimate it to be 40–50 cm to the shoulder, head lower, and about 1 m in length not including the tail. I went into the field to feed the horses and noticed they were acting very excitedly (they are very used to dogs), bucking and cantering around the field and not (as is usual) cantering across a small bridge to get their dinner. On walking towards the bridge I saw, about 50 m away, a large, panther-like creature run between myself and the horses and disappear into dense, swampy woods. It was a grass surface so unfortunately there were no tracks. This animal has been seen on previous occasions by my wife and my neighbour, but this was the first time for me (no longer sceptical). I informed DEFRA.'

28 April 2006

The *Dorset Echo* reported: 'James Barnes claims he saw a panther-like animal while he was sat on a coach as it travelled along the A31. The animal "wandered" across a field next to the dual carriageway at 7 p.m. James said he immediately knew that it was not a domestic cat as the animal was near a group of ponies which helped him scale its size.'

August 2006

Jonathan McGowan reported: 'John Kingswell was driving to work at 6.30 a.m., just as it was getting light, and noticed a roe deer standing on its own in the corner of a passing field. It was staring at something, and as he drove past the hedge a large black cat strode across the road in front of the car. The witness said: "It didn't even look at me, it knew where it was going. It went through the gateway of the opposite maize field. It was about the size of a Labrador, or just a bit smaller."'

❧ Winterbourne Abbas

Date not reported

I received a second-hand report of a sighting by a game keeper out fox shooting one night using a lamp. He was in a hide in a tree and turned on his light when he heard a noise and lit up a big cat. Its eyes shone white/red and he thinks it was black, though he could not be sure in the darkness. Paw prints were found in a muddy gateway on that land some months later, and he assumed from that that it was still around.

 Wool

Bovington Camp – 2002

In 2002 an army officer was alarmed to see a large black cat at Bovington Camp, only about 50 m from housing. It was about 100 yards from him, opposite Monkey World, and he estimated that in height it would have come up to his thigh. Around the same time another witness reported seeing a similar animal in Bovington Camp Wood. It was described as 'black, Great Dane-sized, and with chain around its neck'.

Dorset Gliding Club – 9 September 2003

Lindsay Harris sent this report: 'I thought you'd like to know of a big cat sighting last night near Wool, Dorset. Seen by two of us (both adults of a sceptical nature!) at about 11.45 p.m., heading south on the road between Bere Regis and Wool. My friend Mike and me had been visiting some mutual friends who were staying for the weekend in their caravan at Dorset Gliding Club. That particular evening we had something to eat whilst sat around an open fire and left at 11.45 p.m. At this time of night there was no other traffic around and there are no street lights in the area. We had only been driving for about 1 minute or so in total and had not long turned out from the Gliding Club road onto the main Bere Regis to Wool Road, in the direction of Wool, when something crossed the road in front of us. The car headlights illuminated a largish animal, which was crossing from our right-hand side to the left-hand side of the road. This would mean that it was going into land at the bottom of Dorset Gliding Club. The animal was fawn-coloured, about Alsatian sized or slightly smaller perhaps, though of a heavier build. I didn't see its eyes – it wasn't looking at us as it was sideways on and intent on getting into the hedge – but I did notice the tail in particular which was long and upturned at the end. The animal was typically feline in its gait and was neither running nor creeping, but walking steadily. When we saw it, it was just in range of our headlights, so must have been anywhere between about 15 and 30 yards away. However, my headlights were badly adjusted, meaning that you couldn't see very far ahead in pitch dark! That is why I estimate it could have been as close as 15 yards. I remember quite clearly what I said to my friend: "Er, what was that?" and he said, "Well, I know what I think it was!" We both agreed that it was a big cat of some kind – either a cougar or lioness perhaps. Just a little bit down from there was quite a bit of rubbish strewn over the road, as if recently ransacked by something.'

Winfrith – 10 December 2004

The *Dorset Echo* reported: 'A pensioner was left terrified after she encountered a huge black cat while out walking her dog. Julia Gibson and her mongrel Eden were going across heathland near their home in Winfrith when the incident happened yesterday afternoon. They were walking round a small hill when Eden suddenly chased after what looked like a large black cat. It immediately fled away, climbed a tree and lay along a high branch. Julia got to the dog, saw the animal in the tree and called Eden away to safety. She phoned her husband Dennis for help, but as soon as the dog left the tree the animal ran off across fields in the direction of Owermoigne. Julia said: "It certainly shook me up a bit. I just tried to get Eden away because I thought it might kill the dog. I didn't think of myself at the time and I didn't start shaking until I phoned Dennis. I'm taking a strong cup of tea to steady my nerves." She added that the creature she saw had pure black fur. "It was long and sleek, and very quick, very fast." Dennis said: "Eden weighs about 20 lb and is nearly 3 ft long. Julia said the creature was bigger than that." He said it was not the first time that a black panther-like beast had been seen in the area: "One was spotted last year on the Tadnoll road."'

🐾 Yetminster

Beer Hackett – No date available
A large cat-like animal was apparently seen by five witnesses in a wood. Unfortunately no further details are available.

2000 and 2001
The *Western Gazette*, 5 July 2001, reported: 'A Dorset farmer claims that big cats breeding in the wild are killing his sheep. There have been an increasing number of sightings and sheep farmer, John Burbidge of Yetminster, has lost several lambs and a ewe. A few days ago, his mother spotted a large, cat-like animal in a field. He said: "I had just lost a ewe 2 days before. It was about 8.00 a.m., my mother was looking out of the window and this big creature went bounding through the sheep. They ignored it – she could not believe it. It is very evident that they are breeding. There seem to be a lot of them around. I have seen them twice before, but different in colour from this one. I have heard them as well – they sound like a normal cat, but you hear them from about three fields away."

In February, Mr Burbidge, aged 52, found 4-inch animal footprints and saw a big cat at 5.00 a.m. on the road between Holnest and Yetminster, while he was driving to another farm. He said, "The animal was standing by the side of the road, just looking

From Western Gazette report by Colette Jackson and correspondent Judy Nash.
(Photo credit: Judy Nash)

at me. It did not move. I could not believe the size of its head. It looked much bigger than a puma. It was quite a frightening sight."

Mr Burbidge lost five lambs at three-day intervals last summer and believes a big cat was to blame. Some other farmers have reported attacks on well-grown lambs. Some have disappeared, but others have had their legs bitten off. It is feared the animals are breeding because the cat sighted recently was a lighter colour than the dark puma-like animals seen around Yetminster last year.

Last November an animal broke a sheep's neck and devoured most of the carcass. This was followed by sightings of a big cat in the Yetminster and Sturminster areas.

Colin King of Petties Farm, Yetminster, and Kevin Trevett of Thornford found a strong shearling ewe savaged at Mr King's farm. Mr King said: "This was no dog kill. It was something very powerful that took her by surprise where she lay at dawn. I check the sheep at least twice a day and they were all fit and well the evening before."

Current Theories

What are these big cats, and where do they come from? There are various theories, all, of necessity, slightly crackpot – and none more so than those that claim not to be. No concrete evidence is generally forthcoming either to prove or disprove them, but they remain part of the rich phenomenology of the subject. Below is a brief summary of some of the main ones, with their pros and cons.

The releases theory

The most often quoted reason for the presence of big cats at large in the British landscape is that their owners released them when the Dangerous Wild Animals Act came in in 1976. This Act obliged owners to buy licences for their animals, and undergo welfare and safety inspections. The widespread belief is that unscrupulous owners simply released their big cats rather than pay the money.

Pros
- It sounds a reasonable idea.
- A puma has been caught. One puma has been trapped so far, in Scotland, in 1980. 'Felicity' as she was named was one of two released in the Scottish Highlands by an inmate of Dartmoor prison prior to his incarceration, according to him. Although her droppings implied she had been living wild for a while, she was tame and friendly, and became a crowd-puller at a local wildlife park. The decomposing body of another puma was found in remote country by hikers some years later, coincidentally the same year that Felicity died.

Cons
- Lack of evidence. Only three other people have claimed personally to have released big cats – three pumas and a panther. A few other reports remain as hearsay despite appeals for people involved to come forward. They would have nothing to lose in so doing, and as releasing wild animals was not at that time a crime they cannot be prosecuted retrospectively. This scarcity of evidence for deliberate releases is in marked contrast to the thousands of anomalous feline animals seen in every part of the UK in the past three decades.
- The types of animal involved. The witnesses generally describe two kinds of animal

– black 'panther' types and brown 'puma' types. However, neither the brown nor the black animals resemble the zoo animals they are allegedly bred from, often exhibiting combinations of colours and shapes not typical of any known species. Virtually none of the big cats seen is ever reported as having the spotted coats of the majority of conventional leopards.

Approximately 80% of the animals seen are jet-black, while another 15% conform roughly to the sandy/gingery-brown colours typical of a puma. Five percent show a combination of other colours unobtainable in the wild in their native countries, including pure white. Yet witnesses are commendably resolute: they refuse to alter their testimony to make their sightings conform to the conventional appearance of known big cat species.

The greatest puzzle is the number of black big cats seen. Theorists are reluctant to admit that these can only be melanistic (black) leopards, popularly termed 'black panthers', because of all the big cats the leopards are the most dangerous to man. Yet no black puma has ever been officially recorded, even in its native America.

- There are other anomalies concerning the movement of supposed escaped or released animals. For instance, how did two black panthers turn up separately on the Isle of Mull, seen 20 years apart, bearing in mind the maximum life-span of these animals would be about 15 years?

The escapes theory

Proponents of the escapes theory offer evidence of a large number of animals kept in menageries and circuses, from Roman times up to the early years of the twentieth century: ramshackle institutions from which big cats could theoretically have escaped into the countryside in sufficient numbers to form a breeding population. This existing population, so the theory goes, could then have been topped-up in modern times by deliberately released animals.

Pros

- Dorset has a history of big cats being kept at a variety of sites in the past 150 years. Moreover there are reports of numerous menageries' visits to Dorset, mainly in Victorian times, but going back as early as 1806.
- A lynx of unknown origin was caught by police in the 1990s. The fact that the capture took place in London suggests that the animal could have escaped rather than been deliberately released.

Cons

- The inevitably fruitless hunts. The escapes theory is, like the releases theory, still speculative. Despite their best efforts, its proponents can find no evidence that animals were either released or escaped in more than minute numbers. There have been large-scale police hunts and army stake-outs on many occasions over the past four decades, but neither they nor private hunters and trappers nor farmers' vigils have so far managed to catch or kill one of these panther-like or puma-like big cats.

Conversely, known escapees are usually quickly caught. The record for a known escapee living at large in the wild is, allegedly, about 7 months: this was a clouded leopard that had escaped from Howlett's Zoo in Kent and was shot by a farmer whose sheep it was attacking.

Fortean commentators on the British big cat phenomenon have long noted the ubiquity of accounts of overturned circus vans accompanying cat-flaps (as a rash of sightings is called). None of these tales is ever substantiated, and they are generally reckoned to have the status of urban myths.

The hide-out theory

This is the intriguing idea that UK big cats are a relict species of pre-Ice Age big cats, hiding out in the wild. They are said to be native to Britain, but they are yet to be discovered and named by science. The theory originated in the work of the Belgian cryptozoologist Dr Bernard Heuvelmans and has some adherents in the UK, such as Di Francis, the author of *Cat Country*. However, it is more popular in the USA among such distinguished researchers as Loren Coleman and where the huge wildernesses of that country make it an almost viable proposition.

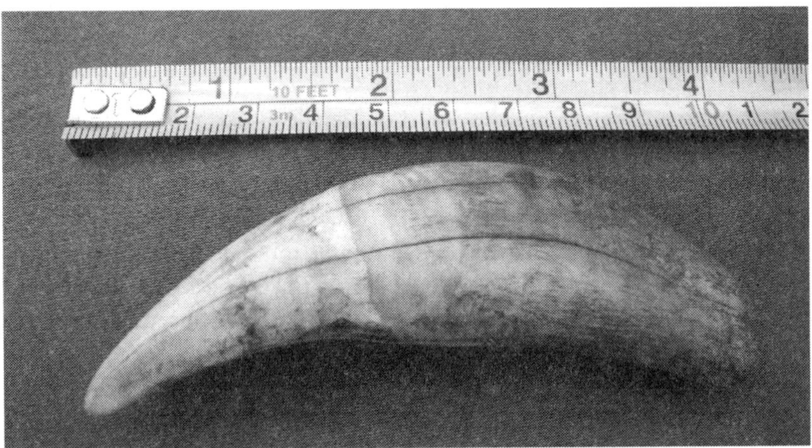

Found in a garden in Stour Row, near Shaftesbury. A lower left canine tooth from a big cat, probably a tiger, estimated to be approximately 10,000 years old. Authenticated by the Natural History Museum, 15 November 2000. The Museum concluded that it had likely been kept for some time as a trophy or talisman owing to its smooth appearance. (Courtesy of Mr Chinchen)

Pros
- It is supported by the evidence in that it accounts for the variability in the cats' colours and appearance.
- Lynxes were native to our islands up until Roman times or even later (they still exist in Europe) and animals bearing some of the characteristics of standard lynxes are

regularly seen here today.

One of the useful features of this theory is the light it casts on taxonomy, showing how rare is scientific consensus on fringe species. It cites examples of animals, such as the okapi, which were well-known in folklore and to native witnesses long before Western scientific zoology recognised them.

Cons

- It is difficult to picture the survival processes involved when so many other comparable species – e.g. wolves – died out.

The hybrid theory

Some researchers have hoped that the variations in the British big cats' colours, sizes and shapes could be accounted for by different species cross-breeding.

Pros

- There is some evidence – in the form of eyewitness reports – of differently coloured animals, and therefore presumably of different species, seen together. Sandy-coloured puma-like cats have been recorded in close proximity to black panther-like animals and therefore, theoretically, could be inclined to mate.

Cons

- It does not happen elsewhere in the wild. One definition of species is that the offspring of two different species will be infertile – like mules. However, some species are close enough both genetically and in size to hybridise successfully, such as the Scottish Wildcat and the domestic cat.

  This is not the case with big cats. Hybrids have been artificially created in zoo conditions, but the practice is considered morally dubious. Specifically the crossing of a leopard and puma has been managed only once, and of the short-lived and dwarfish progeny, one became a stuffed exhibit in Tring Museum. It can be seen at the website www.messybeast.com. This excellent site also assesses the statistical likelihood of viable hybrids and shows photographs of some of the sad, sterile hybrids produced as freak shows in the past.

The absence of bodies and clear photos is a common argument against all the foregoing theories. The bodies of various exotic cats have turned up as road-kills, or they have been shot in error by farmers, but these have always turned out to be the smaller species such as the 'Jungle cat', 'Leopard cat' or 'Swamp cat'. It is doubtful whether these small species can be responsible for sightings of large panther-like or puma-like animals.

Big cats are relatively easy to photograph in their native countries: in Britain they seem well nigh impossible to capture clearly on film or video. There is a handful of photos and some video footage of big cats in Britain, and while many show animals with unmistakably big-cat-like features, none shows anything David Attenborough would look twice at.

Both the hybrid and hide-out theories are more or less inadequate as explanations of the presence of strange feline animals among us; but they fit together. They are based on the same idea – that of a hidden inheritance waiting to be discovered. However, while the hybrid theory sites the treasure at a microscopic level, beneath the skin of individuals' familiar appearances, the hide-out theory sees it on a macroscopic level, concealed in the surrounding landscape. Perhaps they are both best appreciated as modern reworkings of the myth of Demeter – an atavistic sense that half the story is always hidden from us; half the world is in darkness.

Fringe theories

There is an assortment of theories that surface and submerge again at different times, and which are often interesting and sometimes reasonable – but remain unverifiable. Here are some:

Mutant genes

A quasi science-fictional idea is that given 'a limited gene pool', such as the escaped pumas and panthers in Britain are supposed to represent, mutants will spontaneously occur which differ dramatically from their parents; for example normal pumas will become black.

Cat baiting

Another theory is that cat baiting has replaced badger baiting in some criminal fraternities, and big cats are imported and secretly bred for that reason, and then released when they become injured or difficult to maintain; another similar idea is that these animals are bred like lurchers to hunt deer for their owners.

Big feral moggies

A popular misconception is that feral domestic cats can grow to a huge size. In actual fact, owing to a limited diet and having to expend more energy in catching it, feral domestic cats are usually smaller than their stay-at-home counterparts.

Black Dogs

Folklorists and others have speculated that the black big cats may be the ubiquitous 'Black Dogs' of English folklore in a new, modern form. Hide-out theorists contend, conversely, that the Black Dogs of old might have been misperceived Black Cats all along.

Cover up

One theory maintains that the government knows all about these animals and where they come from, but fear insurance claims if they acknowledge their existence. Its proponents claim that people resembling DEFRA officials sometimes remove evidence such as sheep kills ostensibly for examination but actually to smother speculation.

Tulpas

Common in other circles is the belief that these big cat-like animals could be 'thought-forms' or 'tulpas' materialised by practitioners of Tibetan Buddhist religious techniques. Other occult practices, too, are credited with the ability to invoke materialised apparitions.

Daimons

My own personal favourite is the idea that most big cats are native daimons, as the ancient Greeks called them (NB *not* 'demons'). Past British daimons have included the Lambton Worm, goblins, Robin Goodfellow, The Barguest, fairies, Cat Anna, piskies, elves, Black Dogs, brownies, lake monsters, etc. Katherine Briggs, in her book *A Dictionary of Fairies*, names hundreds of them. They are real but intermediate creatures, half in this world and half in the otherworld. They are concrete, but only temporarily so. All the anomalies surrounding Britain's big cats are made intelligible in this context. But why they should appear in this form, and why now, is a deeper mystery. The most illuminating work on the subject of daimons and their philosophical implications is *Daimonic Reality: A Field Guide to the Otherworld*, by my brother, Patrick Harpur.

Variants of all the above ideas also crop up in other areas of anomaly research.

Reappearances

From their studies of other anomalous animals, as well as the Surrey Puma and subsequent ABCs, the distinguished Fortean writers John Michell and Robert Rickard have, they write in *Phenomena: A Book of Wonders*, 'brewed a theory, which, like all our theories is temporarily and loosely held.'

> 'It is that creatures now extinct which once inhabited a certain district continue after their extinction to haunt that district in phantom form, varied with occasional real, physical appearances, until the time comes to re-establish themselves.'

They point to the reappearance of the Bermuda petrel after 300 years of apparent extinction, and in Britain the renaissance of the wild boar. 'There were wild boars and large toothed "tigers" in Pleistocene Britain, and probably more recently', they point out, 'and when Surrey is no more and the commuter train no longer runs to London Bridge, perhaps there will be again'.

Beast of the Vale – painted by Dorset wildlife artist Aviva Halter-Hurn, after a sighting in Broadoak, Marshwood

Select Bibliography

Alderson Smith, Peter (1987) *W.B. Yeats and the Tribes of Danu*. Colin Smythe, Gerrards Cross.

At the Edge. Archive of articles available online, sponsored by Heart of Albion Press. http://www.indigogroup.co.uk/edge/.

Bardens, Dennis (1987) *Psychic Animals*. Robert Hale, London.

Beer, Trevor (1983) *The Beast of Exmoor: Fact or Legend?* Countryside Productions, Barnstable.

Bord, Janet and Colin (1985) *Alien Animals*. Panther Books, London.

Brierly, Nigel (1989) *They Stalk by Night: The Big Cats of Exmoor and the South-West*. Yeo Valley Productions, Bishops Nympton.

Briggs, Katharine M. (1959) *The Anatomy of Puck*. Routledge and Keegan Paul, London.

Briggs, K.M. (1967) *The Fairies in Tradition and Literature*. Routledge and Kegan Paul, London.

Briggs, Katharine M. (1976) *A Dictionary of Fairies*. Penguin, London.

Clark, Jerome (1993) *Unexplained!* Visible Ink Press, Washington, DC.

Coleman, Loren (1983) *Mysterious America*. Paraview, New York.

Croker, T. Crofton (1852) *Fairy Legends and Traditions of the South of Ireland*. John Murray, London.

Crowe, Catherine (1848) *The Night Side of Nature*. George Routledge and Sons, London.

Dash, Mike (1997) *Borderlands*. Arrow Books, London.

David-Neel, A. (1976) *Magic and Mystery in Tibet*. Picador, London.

Eitel, Ernest J. (1984) *Feng Shui: The Science of Sacred Landscape in Old China*, 4th edition. Synergetic Press, Santa Fe.

Evans Wentz, W.Y. (1981) *The Fairy Faith in Celtic Countries*. Colin Smythe, Gerrards Cross.

Fort, Charles (1974) *The Complete Books of Charles Fort*. Dover, New York.

Francis, Di (1983) *Cat Country: The Quest for the British Big Cat*. David and Charles, Newton Abbot.

Fraser, Mark (ed.) (2007) *Big Cats in Britain Yearbook 2006*. CFZ Press, Bideford.

Glassie, Henry (1985) *Irish Folk-Tales*. Penguin, London.

Gregory, Augusta (1979) *Visions and Beliefs in the West of Ireland*. Colin Smythe, Gerrards Cross.

Guggisberg, C.A.W. (1975) *Wild Cats of the World*. David and Charles, Newton Abbot.

Harpur, Merrily (2006) *Mystery Big Cats*. Heart of Albion Press, Loughborough.

Harpur, Patrick (2000) *Daimonic Reality: A Field Guide to the Otherworld*. Penguin, London, and Idyll Arbor, Ravensdale, Washington.

Harpur, Patrick (2003) *The Philosophers' Secret Fire: A History of the Imagination*. Penguin, London, and Ivan R. Dee, Chicago.

Harte, Jeremy (2004) *Explore Fairy Traditions*. Heart of Albion Press, Loughborough.

Harte, Jeremy (1986) *Cuckoo Pounds and Singing Barrows: Folklore of Ancient Sites in Dorset*. Dorset Natural History and Archaeological Society, Dorchester.

Heuvelmans, Bernard (1995) *On the Track of Unknown Animals*. Kegan Paul International, London.

Keel, John A. (2002) *The Complete Guide to Mysterious Beings*. Tor, New York.

Keightley, Thomas (1870) *The Fairy Mythology: Illustrative of the Romance and Superstition of Various Countries*. Available online at http://www.sacred-texts.com/neu/celt/tfm/index.htm.

Kirk, Robert (1976) T*he Secret Common-Wealth of Elves, Fauns and Fairies*. D.S. Brewer for the Folklore Society, London.

Legg, Rodney (1996) *Witches of Dorset*. Dorset Publishing, Wincanton.

Legg, Rodney (1998) *Mysterious Dorset*. Dorset Publishing, Wincanton.

Mac Manus, Diarmuid (1973) *The Middle Kingdom: The Faerie World of Ireland*. Colin Smythe, Gerrards Cross.

Mac Manus, Diarmuid (1979) *Between Two Worlds: True Irish Ghost Stories*. Colin Smythe, Gerrards Cross.

MacRitchie, David (1893) *Fians, Fairies and Picts*. Kegan Paul, Trench, Trubner and Co., London.

McEwan, Graham J. (1986) *Mystery Animals of Britain and Ireland*. Robert Hale, London.

Michell, John and Rickard, Robert (1977) *Phenomena: A Book of Wonders*. Thames and Hudson, London.

Newland, Robert (2006) *Dark Dorset Fairies*. SB Publications, Seaford.

Newland, Robert J. and North, Mark J. (2003) *Dark Dorset Tales of Mystery, Wonder and Terror*. CFZ Press, Bideford.

Roberts, Andy (1986) *Cat Flaps! Northern Mystery Cats*. Brigantia Books, Brighouse.

Shuker, Karl P.N. (1989) *Mystery Cats of the World*. Robert Hale, London.

Tongue, Ruth L. (1965) *Somerset Folklore*. The Folklore Society, London.

Trubshaw, Bob (ed.) (2005) *Explore Phantom Black Dogs*. Explore Books, Heart of Albion Press, Loughborough.

Wade, Chris *Walking with Ghosts in Abbotsbury*. http://www.abbotsbury-heritage.org.uk/results/wade/AbbGhost.htm.

Williams, Charles (1931) *The Place of the Lion*. Faber, London.

Wood-Martin, W.G. (1902) *Traces of the Elder Faiths in Ireland. A Folklore Sketch. A Handbook of Irish Pre-Christian Traditions*. Longmans Green, London.

Yeats, W.B. (1959) *Mythologies*. Macmillan, London.

About Roving Press

The Company – Roving Press is a small publisher producing unusual, distinctive and practical books which give you that little bit extra – more than just a good read. Our titles explore areas and subjects in a down-to-earth way, giving you a real feel for the subjects and places described. If you like exploring, you'll love our books.

The Website – our website (www.rovingpress.co.uk) gives information about our other books, and has special offers from time to time if you would like to place an order for any of our books. We'll also let you know about any special happenings, such as author book signings, talks or other events that might be of interest.

Email – feel free to email us at enquiries@rovingpress.com with any comments, queries or suggestions.

Sightings – if you'd like to contribute a sighting for the next edition of *Roaring Dorset!* or have seen something you're not sure about, log on to Merrily's website – www. dorsetbigcats.org – or email her at research@dorsetbigcats.org.

Other Roving Press Books

A Slice of Apple Pie:
Your One-Stop Guide to Living in America
by Julie Musk

'What on earth are they up to?'

Want to know what life in America is really like? This book is a first-hand account of the experiences of one English family and their dog who lived in the USA for two years. Based largely on life in Ohio, a state known for its middle-American values and as a barometer of the nation (demographers class it as *the* most American state), the author takes an honest, down-to-earth look at America from a British perspective, describing the differences between the two cultures and the reasons behind those differences.

'America is nearly 40 times larger than Britain, 14.3 times larger than France and 2.5 times the size of the European Union, which rather puts things into perspective', the author comments. 'We were exchanging our cosy, rural Dorset existence for a modern suburban home far away ... How would we feel after living in such a different world?'

Travelling to the States can be both exhilarating and downright nerve-racking. By giving you the lowdown on what to expect and how to deal with it, this book offers valuable tips and advice on how to get there and back with your sense of humour intact. Reading it will save you a great deal of time, trouble and money. Moreover, the anecdotes, quotes, cartoons and personal style distinguish it from other travel books. This book is essential reading for anyone curious about life in America.

Published July 2008, 416 pages with illustrations, priced £14.95.
See www.rovingpress.co.uk for more details.

Lesser Known Guides

If you like exploring, you'll love our guides

Want to see what most visitors miss, gain a different perspective and have a few stories to tell?

How would you like to have your own local guide to show you around? Our *Lesser Known Guides* will provide a new way of looking at and exploring specific places, rather than whole areas, with the detail to guarantee you get the most out of your visit.

We want to surprise you, by exploring somewhere in a unique and personal way. We will use local people, contemporary events, local history and the natural world as our basis, while endeavouring to give a snapshot of real life – past and present.

Lesser Known Guides will:

- be unique and informative;
- show you often-overlooked aspects;
- include narrative tales, i.e. real stories;
- encourage you to revisit favourite haunts, to see them in a new light;
- support the local economy and eco-friendly tourism;
- be relevant to children, young people and families;
- include a canine slant to make them dog friendly;
- above all, be easy to read and fun to take out with you.

Our first **Lesser Known Guide to Swanage** should be available in late 2008.

We welcome suggestions for other *Lesser Known Guides*, so please let us know if you have a memory full of stories or an attic full of clippings, which you think will appeal.